W9-BJM-896

IF
THERE'S
A GOD,
WHY
ARE
THERE
ATHEISTS?

R.C. Sproul

If there's a God, why are there atheists?

*

WHY ATHEISTS BELIEVE IN UNBELIEF

Tyndale House Publishers, Inc.
WHEATON, ILLINOIS

Special thanks are in order for the many friends
who contributed to the completion of this book.
My gratitude is extended particularly to Mrs.
William Chevalier, Mrs. Thomas Quarry, and Miss
Mary Semach for assistance in preparing the
manuscript.

Scripture quotations are from the *New American
Standard Bible,* copyright 1960, 1962, 1963, 1971,
1973 by The Lockman Foundation.

This is a revised edition of the book *The
Psychology of Atheism,* first published by Bethany
House.

Second Tyndale House printing, February 1989

Library of Congress Catalog Card Number 88-71946
ISBN 0-8423-1565-9

To

Dr. John H. Gerstner

TEACHER

COUNSELOR

FRIEND

a burning and a shining light

CONTENTS

PREFACE

A chronic complaint among scholars is that a man oversteps the bounds of his discipline by commenting on matters outside it. Often this complaint is valid and needs to be registered. However, it is important to remember that no major field of investigation is so specialized that it never touches other domains. Though a specialist in theology would be presumptuous to speak dogmatically about every aspect of psychology, it would be irresponsible for him to remain silent about those aspects that touch heavily on theology. The question of man's attitude toward God certainly touches psychology. However, it is also a question of great theological importance. This book examines some of the motivating factors of the human mind with respect to God from a theological perspective.

A common charge leveled against people with religious beliefs in general, and with Christian convictions in particular, is that their beliefs are motivated not by reasonable evidence but by psychological needs. This charge calls for an *apologetic* in the classical sense of the word. That is, the charge is worthy of a "reply" or "defense." This book represents an effort to provide such a reply for

Christianity. It is important to note, however, that though this book belongs to the broad category of apologetics, it does not represent a comprehensive defense of the Christian faith. It is not my purpose to present evidence for the existence of God or to provide a total defense of Christianity. Rather the purpose is limited to the issue of psychological motivations. It is my contention that this issue must be dealt with before any sober analysis of the evidence for the Christian faith can be undertaken. This book should be considered an introduction to apologetics in the broad sense.

The central thesis of this book is this: The Christian God has some "attractive" features that might incline a person to embrace God as a narcotic to help him face the threatening character of life, but these are overwhelmingly outweighed by the trauma of encountering God. Though man may desire and create for himself a deity who meets his needs and provides him with innumerable benefits, he will not instinctively desire a God who is holy, omniscient, and sovereign.

If this book is read by one who disclaims belief in God, I can only ask for an honest and open hearing of the case. May there be a guarded truce at least until the issue of psychological bias is dealt with, so that room may be provided for an open debate on the objective evidence for or against the existence of God.

R. C. SPROUL

PART ONE

The Battlefield: Belief and Unbelief

CHAPTER 1
THE GREAT DEBATE

There is no issue that provokes more controversy than the question of whether or not there is a God. The debate is not limited to the parlor or the marketplace but has been the focal point of massive intellectual endeavor for centuries. The debate raged in the ancient world as vigorously as it does today. The Epicureans scoffed at the Stoics for their theistic beliefs. The Skeptics mocked the Platonists' "Idea of the Good" and the Aristotelians' "Unmoved Mover." Not all nations were enamored or persuaded by Israel's Yahweh. In every culture with believers in God there have been unbelievers. In no sense can we say there has ever been universal acceptance of either theism or atheism.

The debate has sometimes been calm, sometimes brutal. The Inquisition, the rack, the sword, and the bullet have been used as means of persuasion for religious points of view. People have been banished from their families for changing their religious alliances. Men fight, maim, and kill—or yawn dispassionately between casual puffs of their pipes as the issue is discussed. In one culture the killing of the infidel—or the believer—is viewed as a work of merit, while another culture proclaims that people should never get excited over religion. From apathy to violence, from unbridled passion to careful, calculated reasoning, the debate takes place.

VARIETIES OF THEISM

The word *theism* is an extremely difficult one to define. It is a general term that includes a wide variety of species. Literally, the word means "Godism," that is, belief in God. It is derived from *theos,* the Greek word for God. The content of the term, however, is far more difficult to isolate than its derivation. One dictionary defines *theism* as follows: "belief in the existence of a god or gods."[1] If we check further in the dictionary to the entry *god,* we read, "a being or object believed to have more than natural attributes and powers and to require man's worship" and also "a person or thing of supreme value."[2] This definition is broad in scope and serves to increase the ambiguity that so often surrounds the meaning of the word *God.*

Because of the ambiguity of the word *God* and because of the multitude of meanings attached to it, some contemporary thinkers have despaired of having any meaningful discussion of the word at all. There is a crisis of language in the whole area of God-talk.[3] Perhaps this can be illustrated by the now famous parable of Anthony Flew.

Once upon a time two explorers came upon a clearing in the jungle. In the clearing were growing many flowers and many weeds. One explorer says, "Some gardener must tend this plot." The other disagrees. "There is no gardener." So they pitch their tents and set a watch. No gardener is ever seen. "But perhaps he is an invisible gardener." So they set up a barbed wire fence. They electrify it. They patrol with bloodhounds. . . . But no shrieks ever suggest that some intruder has received a shock. No movement of the wire ever betrays an invisible climber. The bloodhounds never give cry. Yet still the Believer is not convinced. "But there is a gardener, invisible, intangible, insensible to electric shocks, a gardener who has no scent and makes no sound, a gardener who comes secretly to look after the garden which he loves." At last the Skeptic despairs, "But what is left of your original assertion? Just how does what you call an invisible, intangible, eternally elusive gardener differ from an imaginary gardener or even from no gardener at all?"

Flew concludes, "A fine brash of hypothesis may thus be killed by inches, the death of a thousand qualifications."[4] In other words, the gardener—or God—cannot be discussed seriously unless people agree on what sort of being they are attempting to discuss.

The contemporary mind has located the problem in terms of language. Some have concluded that the word *God* is a meaningless symbol and is incapable of being discussed rationally. Such radical skepticism, however, is an overreaction to the problems involved. Though the word *God* abounds with linguistic difficulties, it still functions in a meaningful way in our society. Though the ideas surrounding the word are often vague and hazy, and though the word has a multitude of meanings, it is not totally meaningless. Most people still assume that *God* refers to some person, or power, on a level of existence different from ordinary humanity. *Theism* is, it is generally agreed, belief that such a power or being exists.

Before proceeding further with a consideration of theism, let us look at the various categories of it.

Polytheism. This term has specific reference to number. That is, polytheism is a kind of theism that affirms the existence of many gods. These deities may vary in gender, status, authority, and job description. The number of gods included in a polytheistic system can vary from two to infinity. Hinduism, for example, has hundreds of gods, as do most nature religions around the world.

Henotheism. Henotheism represents a peculiar kind of theism. It is something between polytheism and monotheism. Simply stated, henotheism is defined as geographical, ethnic, or national monotheism. That is, a particular nation or group believes in one God who reigns exclusively over them, within the limits of their territorial borders. Other gods exist and reign over other nations. The existence of many gods (polytheism) is affirmed, but allegiance is given to one alone. Henotheism differs from monotheism in that the God worshiped is not universal in his dominion. In some cultures, henotheism represented a transitional state between the movement from polytheism to monotheism.[5]

Monotheism. Strictly speaking, monotheism simply refers to the belief in one universal deity. Radically different descriptions of that one deity may be offered. The one deity may be regarded as personal or impersonal, transcendent or immanent, abstract or concrete, finite or infinite, and so on. The term *monotheism* is usually associated in the Western world with the Judeo-Christian tradition, including Islam. However, monotheism in the sense defined is not limited to that tradition. Other religions have also held to the belief in one God. And many people who profess no particular religion at all claim they believe in one transcendent, all-powerful Being called God. In fact, it is probably safe to say that most people, at least in the Americas and Europe, believe either in one God or no god at all. (This situation may be changing with some of the increasingly popular forms of spirituality and occultism.) Polytheism and henotheism are not live options for most people nowadays. To be a believer means, generally, to believe in one God. The only viable alternatives are atheism and agnosticism.

ATHEISM AND AGNOSTICISM

Atheism. In a technical sense atheism is not quite as difficult to define as are the varieties of theism. Atheism involves the rejection of any form of theism. To be an atheist is to disavow belief in any kind of god or gods. However, in the function of language, the term has often been employed to signify a rejection or disavowal of a particular god or group of gods. For example, the early Christians were sometimes called atheists because they rejected the popular deities of Rome. Likewise, the term *atheism* has been employed by many Christian thinkers in dealing with other religions. Religions that are in opposition to Christianity have been called atheistic insofar as they were understood to be worshiping false gods. This approach, whether it comes from a Christian, a Muslim, or from any other source, is usually founded on the premise that the worship of a false god is the worship of no god.

A classic example of this use of the term *atheist* can be seen in the record of the trial of the aged Bishop Polycarp as he stood in the Roman arena in the second century.

And when finally he was brought up, there was a great tumult on hearing that Polycarp had been arrested. Therefore, when he was brought before him, the proconsul asked him if he were Polycarp. And when he confessed that he was, he tried to persuade him to deny (the faith), saying, "Have respect to your age"—and other things that customarily followed this, such as, "Swear by the fortune of Caesar; change your mind; say, 'Away with the atheists!'" But Polycarp looked with earnest face at the whole crowd of lawless heathen in the arena and motioned to them with his hand. Then groaning and looking up to heaven, he said, "Away with the atheists."[6]

Needless to say, Polycarp burned at the stake.

Agnosticism. This term refers to a lack of conviction with respect to the question of theism. Technically considered, agnosticism is a variety of atheism. If theism is considered to signify the assertion of the existence of one or more gods and a-theism means non-theism, then the agnostic is, properly speaking, an atheist. That is, if a-theism or non-theism includes everything outside of the category of theism, then agnosticism must be included, since it lacks any positive assertion of theism. However, the term *agnosticism* is rarely employed as a synonym for atheism. Rather, the agnostic seeks to declare neutrality on the issue, desiring to make neither assertion nor denial of the theistic question. The term derives from the Greek *agnosis,* meaning "without knowledge." The agnostic maintains that there is insufficient knowledge upon which to make an intellectual judgment about theism. He prefers to suspend judgment until such time that more available data will incline him either to affirm or deny the existence of a god or gods.

Many believers and atheists consider agnosticism to be a great intellectual cop-out, since the agnostic avoids passing judgment because (he says) there is insufficient data. Strict theists and atheists say there *is* sufficient data to make a judgment. However, agnostics and those who sympathize with their position say their position is respectable, since they avoid doing any harm in the name of either belief or unbelief. In our contemporary society, where intolerance is often regarded as the supreme evil, agnosticism seems like an attractive option for many people. As we shall see below, however, it does not satisfy man's religious urges.

THE HISTORICAL SITUATION

In terms of numerical statistics, it is safe to say that the vast majority of human beings have at least subscribed to some variety of theism. Theism has been so persistent in human civilization and has been so characteristic of man that it has been fashionable to describe man in terms of being *homo religiosus*. Man appears to be incurably religious.

As religious as the human race is and as numerous as theists are, on the practical level the question becomes more complex. There is always a gap between man's profession of faith and his practice of it. Thus, it is sometimes necessary to distinguish between theoretical atheism and practical atheism.

Practical Atheism. Practical atheism refers to the situation where people profess belief in some kind of deity, but, for all practical purposes, live as if there were no god. If we consider this practical dimension, perhaps the total number of atheists in the world (particularly in the modern world) would be substantially increased.

Countless polls have been taken in the United States to query the populace with reference to theism. Some polls have put the level of adherence to theism as high as 98 percent. Almost all polls have shown that a considerable majority of the American people believe in some kind of god. Further analysis will show, however, that the god people believe in is often so ambiguous as to weaken the significance of the polls.

I witnessed a spontaneous poll of this kind administered to the studio audience of a popular television talk show. This poll was prompted by the obvious frustration the host was experiencing with his guest. The guest was a well-known woman who had distinguished herself by a militant crusade against discrimination against atheists in the U.S. The host and his guest were locked in verbal combat over the issue of the existence of God. To settle the debate, the host resorted to "counting noses" to decide the issue of theism or atheism. He asked the studio audience, "How many of you believe in some kind of higher power?" The response was overwhelmingly affirmative. The noted guest failed to question the wording of the query. What is a "higher power"? Is it energy? Cosmic dust? I was left to wonder what the results of the poll would have been had it been worded differently. I wonder how the vote would have been, for example, if the question were stated, How many of you believe in Yahweh, the God of Old Testament Israel? or, How many of you believe in the triune God of the New Testament?

At the practical level it makes an enormous difference whether one's god is a "studied ambiguity" such as an undefined "higher power," or is a deity with a name, a historical relationship, and moral imperatives. It is one thing to affirm the existence of an "unknown" god who makes no ultimate demands upon one's life. It is quite another matter to affirm the existence of a God who makes an absolute claim on life, who holds people accountable for every deed and thought, and who threatens a person with everlasting torment if he refuses to obey Him.

Thus supporters of atheism can vary in number according to what kind of theism is under question.

Modern Theoretical Atheism. Atheism, as an intellectual

option, received a great boost from the so-called Enlightenment of eighteenth-century Europe. This movement began in England and moved to France and then on to Germany, where it found its fullest expression.

The Enlightenment has been described as a time in which all the forces of skepticism were launched against classical Christian theology. Such a description, however, would be an oversimplification and caricature of this period. The Enlightenment provoked an intense movement of intellectual debate that opened many of the assumptions of former generations to serious question. Indeed, every field of intellectual inquiry was touched by this movement.

One group of thinkers within the framework of the Enlightenment gave an emphatic critique of religion. This group was the French Encyclopedists, so called because they produced a massive intellectual encyclopedia. Ernst Cassirer says of French Encyclopedism that it "declares war openly on religion, on its claims to validity and truth. It accuses religion of having been an eternal hindrance to intellectual progress and of having been incapable of founding a genuine morality and a just social and political order."[7] In the minds of the Encyclopedists, a man is enlightened only when he frees himself from the God-hypothesis in order to open the way to free intellectual progress.

Perhaps the two leading voices of the French Enlightenment, in terms of atheism, were Paul Henri Thiry d'Holbach (who characterized himself as "the personal enemy of God") and Denis Diderot. Both of these thinkers approached atheism from the perspective of natural science.

Holbach argued strenuously against previous rational theories that sought to establish the notion of God on the basis of innate (inborn) knowledge. He argued that the idea of God is not innate and that the widespread belief in God among the masses does not indicate any kind of evidence for God. Holbach maintained that "the universal assent to God's existence may mean nothing more than universal terror before natural calamities together with ignorance of natural laws."[8] Notice that in this critique of the God-hypothesis Holbach introduced a psychological explanation as one possible explanation for the widespread belief in God. Man's terror before the unknown moves him to make the assumption that there is a God. The point Holbach makes is that with the explosion of knowledge in the areas of the natural sciences, man is liberated from the tyranny of the unknown.

Denis Diderot shared Holbach's unbridled optimism in the natural sciences' ability to provide a basis for social, political, and moral order without recourse to a God-hypothesis. God is no longer needed to explain the cause of the natural or moral order. Indeed, the God-hypothesis served only as a hindrance and a barrier to understanding. Both Holbach and Diderot were content with the theory of spontaneous generation to account for the origin of things, and they found the God-hypothesis "scientifically useless." For the Encyclopedists, the idea of God was both unnecessary and undesirable. Man and the world could be adequately explained without recourse to God. Consequently, a closed universe was conceived of, lacking room for intervention from without.[9]

Though the development of the Enlightenment in Germany left its mark of criticism on Christianity, it was not as hostile to theism as much as the French Encyclopedists were. Gotthold Lessing and Johann Herder sought to subordinate revelation to reason and the supernatural to the natural. Again, the clarion call was to intellectual maturity, freedom from dependence upon adolescent fantasies of the supernatural.

The German Enlightenment reached its zenith in the monumental work of Immanuel Kant. Kant was not an enemy of theism, but he rendered a serious attack on the classical arguments for the existence of God. He himself embraced a "functional theism," arguing for the existence of God on moral grounds. In spite of his own theistic position, however, Kant laid the groundwork for future rejections of the idea of God.

In his critique of traditional arguments for the existence of God, Kant attacked the ability to move intellectually from the visible realm of human experience to the spiritual world of God. Since God is beyond the scope of scientific research, He remains unknowable and undemonstrable. The idea of God must be affirmed for practical purposes but can never be verified as a reality. Kant argued on practical grounds, saying, "We must live as though there were a God." God is necessary to insure a meaningful ethic.[10]

It was precisely Kant's idea of practical or functional necessity of theism that was rejected by later thinkers. If knowledge is restricted to the visible realm, there is no need to go beyond that realm. The atheism that manifested itself in terms of nineteenth-century thought saw no need to appeal to a spiritual being who would guarantee meaning for the visible world. The leading atheists of the nineteenth century sought either to find the meaning of existence within the visible world (Marx, Freud) or to reject the thesis of ultimate meaning altogether (Nietzsche).

Twentieth-century atheism has followed largely along the same lines of restricting knowledge to the visible realm. In both existential and analytical philosophy there has been a wholesale abandonment of metaphysical inquiry. Again, theism is viewed as being either undemonstrable or unnecessary.

MODERN THEORETICAL THEISM

The rising crescendo of atheism established along skeptical lines has not gone unopposed. In spite of the Enlightenment's critique of theistic proofs, theism is still very much alive. The drift of theistic belief, however, has been deeply affected by Kant's critique of rational evidence.

The dominant approach to theism in the nineteenth century manifested itself in a heavily immanentistic theology. That is, God was viewed as either part or the whole of the natural realm. This world, not the supernatural realm, became the arena of God. Revelation from above was largely excluded as a basis for theistic belief.

The beginning of the twentieth century saw a massive revolt against the immanentistic drift of the nineteenth-century theology. The work of the Swiss theologian Karl Barth appeared as a protest against immanentism. Barth made a passionate defense of a deity whose transcendence is known only by revelation. Though Barth tenaciously defended a theism of transcendence, he did it within the broad context of Kant's thought. Though he argued for the validity of revelation, he acknowledged that this revelation cannot be demonstrated or authenticated by reason. Consequently theism rests, for Barth, on the foundation of faith rather than reason.[11]

This nonrational approach to theism has been widely adopted in twentieth-century theology. In radically divergent views of theology, the nonrational strand remains intact. From philosopher Karl Jasper's "Final Experience" to liberal theologian Rudolf Bultmann's "punctiliar moment of decision" to the Jesus-freaks' "mind-blowing" encounter, the emphasis has fallen on subjective experience as the basis for theism. There are many Christians who at this moment would claim that they base their belief in God mainly on their own experience of Him. The old hymn ended with the line "You ask me how I know He lives? He lives within my heart!" For many believers that holds true today. We will examine this attitude more closely in the next chapter.

Whatever the intellectual content and foundation for contemporary theism is, the fact remains that belief in God is very much a part of modern culture. Whether the foundations for theism are theoretically valid and defensible or not, the fact of theism persists.

Thus, far into the twentieth century the debate between theists and atheists continues. Why? Why is there not more agreement on this vital issue? How can such brilliant thinkers and competent scholars come to such radically divergent positions?

This is a question that has concerned me

NOTES

1. *Webster's Ninth New Collegiate Dictionary,* s.v. "theism." The definition continues in this way: "*specif:* belief in the existence of one God viewed as the creative source of man and the world who transcends yet is immanent in the world."

2. *Webster's Ninth,* s.v. "god."
3. For a further analysis of the God-talk crisis see Edward Farley, *The Transcendence of God* (Philadelphia: Westminster, 1960), and Helmut Gollwitzer, *The Existence of God as Confessed by Faith,* trans. James W. Leith (Philadelphia: Westminster, 1965).
4. Quoted in Paul M. van Buren, *The Secular Meaning of the Gospel* (New York: Macmillan, 1963), 3, citing *New Essays in Philosophical Theology,* ed. A. Flew and A. MacIntyre (London: SCM, 1955), 96ff.
5. In response to the thesis that the Israelite religion moved in such an evolutionary pattern, see Yehezkel Kaufman, *The Religion of Israel,* trans. Moshe Greenberg (Chicago: University of Chicago Press, 1960).
6. Cyril C. Richardson, ed., *Early Christian Fathers,* vol. 1 of *The Library of Christian Classics* (Philadelphia: Westminster, 1953), 152.
7. Ernst Cassirer, *The Philosophy of the Enlightenment,* trans. Fritz C. A. Koelln and James P. Pettegrove (Boston: Beacon, 1951), 134.
8. James Collins, *God in Modern Philosophy* (Chicago: Gateway, 1967), 151.
9. Ibid., 154.
10. Ibid., 190-200.
11. See John B. Cobb's analysis of Barth in *Living Options in Protestant Theology* (Philadelphia: Westminster, 1962), 171-197.

CHAPTER 2
THE TENSION OF DISAGREEMENT

We have seen that the issue of the existence of God has not been settled once and for all in Western civilization. Great minds have taken opposing positions with reference to this question. Impressive arguments have come forth from the side of atheism and the side of theism. The disagreement has not left all men in a state of dispassionate lack of concern. Rather, the debate continues, often with militant rhetoric. Some have sought to circumvent the heat of the controversy by seeking a third alternative which would give us at least a guarded truce.

The third alternative that has captured the imagination of many Westerners is the alternative of seeing the question of the existence of God as a subjective-practical question rather than an objective-metaphysical question. Thus the question is dealt with on the basis of a subjective evaluation of faith or its denial. In concrete terms, a person may look at it this way: "I believe in God, and my faith in God is meaningful to my life. It brings me comfort. It provides a goal and purpose for my life. It offers hope to me that the universe is ulti-mately meaningful. And because the whole of existence is ultimately meaningful, my individual life is meaningful." On the other hand, a person may say, "I do not believe in God, and

I've found it quite meaningful to live without such faith. So
for me and for my life, there is no God." It is a short step for
these two persons to avoid the controversy of their different
conclusions by saying that for the one who finds faith meaningful, God is true, and for the one who finds unbelief meaningful, God is not true.

Here the question of the existence of God is reduced to a
question of practical meaningfulness in the life of individuals.
If truth is defined as that which is meaningful to the one who
believes, then of course anything that is meaningful to the individual may be regarded as true. Also, anything that is not
meaningful to the individual may be regarded as false.

This approach to the question of the existence of God does
not solve the tension of disagreement. It does serve to soften
the emotional hostility that often surrounds the debate. It
does much to bring us peace, but very little to bring us
truth. The issue of the objective existence of God remains.

The question of God's existence is a different question
from the question of what man finds meaningful and practical.
By taking this third alternative, we can discover many an-
swers to the questions of practical meaningfulness (whatever
that much-abused word *meaning* may actually point to), but
we will not find an answer to the question of the existence of
God. For example, if I believe in God with all of my heart
and with all of my mind and find that belief so meaningful
that I devote my life to serving this God; if I pray to this
God, if I worship this God, if I sacrifice my life to this God,
and in fact there is no such God, all of my praying and devotion and sacrifice will not bring Him into existence. That is, if
I find all kinds of personal meaning by believing in God, that
meaningfulness will not cause a God to be, if in fact there is
no such God. On the other hand, if I do not believe in God
and am convinced that God is the invention of superstitious
minds, and is irrelevant to my existence; if I find my meaning
in life without reference to God and in fact there is a God,
then all of my unbelief and disinterest will not change that

fact. In the final analysis, there either is a God or gods, or there are none. There either is something or someone ultimate apart from me, or there is not.

Not only can the question of the objective existence of God not be decided by personal meaningfulness of the individual, but the question can also not be decided by a collective discovery of subjective meaningfulness of the God hypothesis. That is to say, my individual belief or lack of it cannot decide the ultimate question of the existence of God, nor can a number of individual beliefs decide the ultimate issue. Simply stated, truth is not determined by "counting noses." Such a democratic approach to truth wherein the majority wins can again only be descriptive of what the many believe rather than what actually is. If 99 percent of the people of the world believe in God, that does not mean there is a God. Conversely, if 99 percent of the world believe there is no God, that in itself does not decide the issue. Our culture places much emphasis on democracy and on public opinion polls, but they have little to say in regards to ultimate truth. Ten thousand people on the street can be wrong.

THE LAW OF CONTRADICTION
In the objective realm of the question of the existence of God both sides cannot be right. There cannot be a God, or gods, on the one hand and at the same time be no gods. To avoid the pain of disagreement by affirming both poles is to violate the law of contradiction. The law of contradiction is that A cannot be A and non-A at the same time. That is to say, there cannot be God and no God at the same time. To say that God is and is not is to speak nonsense.

To be sure, the twentieth century has shown a tendency to ignore the law of contradiction as a necessary principle for coherent discourse. In reaction against previous forms of rationalism, many contemporary thinkers, particularly of the existentialist school, have maintained that truth indeed may be contradictory—that is, truth rises above logical categories and cannot be restricted by the law of contradiction. On the other hand, thinkers who have continued to operate using the law of contradiction have been charged with perpetuating Aristotle's system of truth, which can no longer function in modern thought.

It should be made emphatically clear that adherence to the law of contradiction does not presuppose a blind acceptance of the entire system of Aristotle's philosophy. Aristotle did not invent logic, nor was the law of contradiction the conclusion of his system. For Aristotle, logic was defined, not invented. He described logic as being the *organon* of all science and truth-seeking. That is, logic was viewed as a necessary instrument or tool by which knowledge could be coherently expressed and understood.[1] Statements that violated the law of contradiction were judged by Aristotle to be nonsense statements, to be meaningless with respect to content.

Though in the twentieth century we have seen a rejection of the law of contradiction at the theoretical level, we have seen at the same time a virtual universal acceptance of the law of contradiction at the practical level. Though people deny the validity of the law of contradiction intellectually, they all live their daily lives with the assumption that the law is valid. The philosopher who denies the validity of the law of contradiction in his study still adopts the law when he drives his car through an intersection of a highway. When he sees a truck speeding toward the point of the intersection where he wishes to proceed, he stops his car because he knows that if there is a truck in front of him, there cannot at the same time *not* be a truck in front of him. As he thinks his theory of noncontradiction, he applies the brakes in his car.

If a doctor found conclusive evidence for the presence of a malignant cancer in the body of one of his patients and reasoned within himself that there was also *no* cancer in his patient's body and treated the patient on the basis of that possibility, his treatment would be regarded as nothing less than criminal. Man cannot survive without assuming the validity of the law of contradiction.

In the intellectual community there is often a fascination with statements that are blatant violations of the law of contradiction. At first impact, such statements from supposedly intelligent professors often carry the aura of profundity and produce a sense of awe in the bewildered student. For example, I once witnessed a well-known theologian making this statement to his students: "God is absolutely immutable in His essence: God is absolutely mutable in His essence." At the end of this contradictory statement, the professor paused to allow his words to sink in. The reaction of his students was almost reverent. They were filled with awe at the profundity of the professor's statement. When I queried some of the students about what they learned from such a statement, they admitted that they had learned nothing, but that the professor's statement was certainly deep and penetrating. One student remarked, "I cannot understand what the professor is saying. It is too deep for me, but I am sure the professor must understand it because he is so much more brilliant than I am."

A further example may be drawn from my own experience as a professor of philosophy. On one occasion I stood before my class and held a piece of chalk in my hand. I said to the class, which included on that particular afternoon the dean of the school as he sat in to audit my class, "This piece of chalk is not a piece of chalk." I made the statement in a tone of voice that was somewhat hushed and awe-inspired, the kind of voice a professor might use when he is trying to communicate something deep. I screwed up my face to make myself appear contemplative and pensive. After the statement, I asked the students, "What did you learn from that statement?" After some careful consideration, one student answered by saying, "That piece of chalk is not *really* a piece of chalk." I responded, "What piece of chalk?" and the student said, "That piece of chalk." I said, "But this piece of chalk is not a piece of chalk, so why do you call it a piece of chalk?"

At this point the student became befuddled and an atmosphere of confusion permeated the room.

After a further period of silent contemplation, the dean became involved in the inquiry by stating, "I have learned that that *particular* piece of chalk that you have in your hand is not a piece of chalk." I said, "Which particular piece of chalk?" He indicated the piece of chalk I had in my hand and I replied, "I told you this piece of chalk is not a piece of chalk. Why do you insist on calling it a piece of chalk?" Finally, after much frustration that was moving toward the level of annoyance, a black urban pastor could stand the intellectual nonsense no longer. He boldly declared, "Man, I ain't learned nothin'!" Needless to say, I was relieved to discover that there was at least one thinking creature left in the room. In some circumstances the bold declaration and profession of both sides of a contradiction may sound clever or profound, but upon closer scrutiny the contradiction seems merely absurd.

The law of contradiction is not a system of truth, it is not a self-contained philosophy, it is not even a theory of knowledge. It is simply what Aristotle called it—an instrument of meaningful discourse, an instrument necessary for verbal communication to be understood. The law of contradiction cannot, in and of itself, prove the existence of God nor, of course, could it disprove the existence of God. The service rendered to us at this point by the law of contradiction is simply this: It demonstrates to us that we cannot solve the tension of disagreement by affirming both poles. One side must be wrong; both sides cannot be right. Much as we moderns want to "have it both ways" in the name of freedom and tolerance, it cannot be done. A flight into nonrationality only adds to the dilemma of the classical issue. The disagreement remains, and we move then to the question of why the disagreement remains. How is it possible for men of equal brilliance, of equal intellectual prowess, of equal educational backgrounds and sophistication to arrive at two mutually exclusive conclusions?

REASONS FOR DISAGREEMENT
ABOUT OBJECTIVE TRUTH

When experts disagree and come to mutually exclusive conclusions, the layman normally concludes that the problem
simply cannot be solved. In reality, however, it is quite possible that one set of conclusions may in fact be correct while
the other is in error. It is also possible that the expert who
comes to the right conclusion has come to that conclusion as
much through good fortune as through good reasoning. That
is, it is possible that the expert who has come to the wrong
conclusion has been more consistent in his reasoning than the
expert who arrives at the correct conclusion.

Experts, of course, are capable of making mistakes. The
greatest minds are subject to error. There are innumerable
ways in which errors are made in the process of rational debate. A considerable number of factors may be involved that
will lead to error. For purposes of simplification, we can list
four basic kinds of errors that are frequently made by the
greatest of men. The four ways in which errors are made
and by which disagreement comes are the following:

1. Epistemological errors
2. Formal errors in reasoning
3. Factual errors in empirical investigation
4. Psychological prejudice that distorts conclusions.

EPISTEMOLOGICAL ERRORS

Epistemology is that branch of philosophy that deals specifically with the question of knowledge. It deals with definition
of truth and the methods of attaining truth. There is no uni-
versally accepted epistemology by which experts operate.
Historically there have been many schools of epistemology,
the most famous of which have been the schools of rationalism and empiricism. The various schools of rationalism have
given great emphasis to the function of reasoning in order to
arrive at truth. The accent has fallen upon the formal and
theoretical rather than upon the material and the tangible. In
extreme cases, some from the tradition of rationalism argued

that whatever can be conceived as being true logically must
exist in reality. We can call this school the *conceptualist*
school. That which can be conceived by the mind in rational
categories must exist in reality. The seventeenth-century es-
sentialists were representative of this approach to truth.

On the other hand, the *empiricist* school has sought to
discover truth more through the examination of hard data,
through what is perceived by the five senses, than through
logical speculation. Here the rule is, whatever is perceived by
the senses is true. Whatever cannot be perceived by the
senses is not true. Two experts using these two vastly different approaches to knowledge could easily come to different
conclusions regarding the existence of God. The conceptualist
might argue that to conceive of God is perfectly proper within the context of rational speculation and does not pose immediate problems of irrationality and therefore must be
regarded as being true.[2] On the other hand, one who followed a very strict empirical course of epistemology would
argue that a metaphysical being called God who cannot be
perceived by the senses cannot be true because it cannot
meet the test for truth, that of empirical verification.[3]

We can see how two brilliant minds can come to different
conclusions using two different epistemologies as their basis
for investigation. Of course, it is important to remember that
the two epistemologies mentioned above are by no means
the only epistemologies vying for acceptance among scholars.
Indeed, it would be very unlikely to find many philosophers in
the twentieth century who would take such a one-sided view
of rationalism or such a one-sided view of empiricism as out-
lined above. The conclusion of the theist or the atheist may
be largely conditioned by the validity or invalidity of the epistemology employed.

FORMAL ERRORS

Even if a philosopher uses a perfectly valid epistemology, that
will be no guarantee that the conclusions of his thought will
be equally valid. Though the starting point may be correct, it

is quite possible that errors of reasoning may occur through-out the process of the thought. Though not all philosophers have been rationalists, all philosophers have resorted to some kind of reasoning process to argue their views. This has been demonstrated in existential philosophy as well as other forms of epistemology.

The question of formal truth concerns the question of in-ternal consistency. It involves questions of logic and of state-ments that can be verified or falsified strictly by reason. For example, if a philosopher began with the statement, "All men are mortal," then added the second premise, namely, that "Socrates was a man," and reasoned to the conclusion that "Socrates was *not* a mortal," the philosopher would be mak-ing an obvious blunder. His conclusion would not be valid.

It is interesting that in logic textbooks examples of logical errors are not cited from the lower classes of literature, such as comic books or tabloids or propaganda manuscripts, but from the finest literary products of Western culture. Passages from such brilliant thinkers as John Stuart Mill, David Hume, Immanuel Kant, Aristotle, Cicero, and others are used as illustrations of examples of blatant logical fallacies present in the works of the most learned men.[4]

Thus, a major reason why brilliant men disagree about important issues is because even brilliant men are capable of making mistakes in their reasoning process. When we see experts disagree, we must not assume at the outset that the experts in question have all been consistently reasonable in their formal argumentation.

FACTUAL OR INDUCTIVE ERRORS

Just as men can err in formal reasoning, so mistakes can creep into our thinking by virtue of errors made in collection of hard data. Descartes in his day demonstrated the very real possibility of perception errors made by men. We are aware of the limitations of our sense organs, which cannot grant us total knowledge and accuracy. For example, there are fre-quencies of sound that are so high that they are not audible under normal circumstances to the human ear. This was made painfully clear to me in an incident from my childhood. Having purchased a new puppy, I went to the hardware store to buy a dog whistle. Upon coming home I tested the whistle by blowing it, but I heard no sound. I returned to the store, complained that the whistle did not work, and asked for a refund. The store owner carefully explained to me that though I could not hear the sound of the whistle, my young puppy could and would respond. That was my practical introduction to the difference of sensitivity of perceiving sound between the human ear and the ear of a dog.

The other senses that we possess are also seen to be less in strength and sensitivity than those of other creatures in our own environment. There are animals whose sense of smell is considerably greater than ours, others whose sense of sight is greater, and so on. We have been able to overcome some of the limitations of our senses by the invention of sophisticated and sensitive machinery of measurement and observation. But even these machines cannot be claimed to offer perfect sense perception. Natural limits will always be involved in the empirical process. We simply cannot assume that things invisible or inaudible to us have no existence. The scientists know better, and they also know that there is much that lies beyond the scope of the most technically advanced machines.

Not only are we materially vulnerable to the limits of our sensibilities, but we always face the problem of reaching conclusions on the basis of insufficient data. For example, if a hundred college students ate a dining hall meal and thirty of those students were immediately affected with intestinal distress, we would seek to find the common denominator in their experience in order to isolate the cause of their sickness. If we discovered that seventy of the students had lemon meringue pie for dessert and the other thirty students had cherry pie for dessert and that it was the students that had the cherry pie that were sick, we would probably conclude that the cherry pie caused the intestinal problem.

Suppose, however, the real cause of the sickness was the fact that the student who served the cherry pie was carrying a highly contagious disease, while a different student served the lemon meringue pie, so that the cause of the illness was not the cherry pie; rather, the cherry pie was simply the avenue by which these thirty people came in contact with the real cause of the disease. To simply stop at the cherry pie would be to come to a conclusion with insufficient evidence.

The problem of empirical error is complicated in the realm of negation of existence. It is obviously easier to verify the existence of something empirically than to negate the existence of something empirically. For example, if one made the assertion that there was gold in Alaska, the verification of that statement could conceivably be done very quickly and very simply. Though unlikely, it is possible that the first spade of earth overturned in Alaska would produce gold. If such a happening took place, the original assertion would be verified. However, to negate the assertion that there is gold in Alaska would involve searching every square inch of that land to finally say with certainty there was no gold in Alaska.

Because of this difference in difficulty of verification, many theists have taken comfort that it's virtually impossible to disprove the existence of God by an empirical method. To do so would demand a thorough investigation of every nook and cranny of the entire universe. (And even if such a search were possible, it is also true that we may not possess the perceptual abilities necessary to find an invisible, transcendent Being.) The atheist, of course, has pointed out that he is not seeking to deny the existence of God merely on the basis of empirical data but is arguing that the assertion of the existence of God leaves the burden of proof upon the affirmer rather than upon the denier.

Another subtle problem with inductive research and human fallibility was pointed out in the early stages of the LSD controversy. When a wave of protest arose concerning the experiments conducted by Dr. Timothy Leary at Harvard University, Leary was charged with the improper use of hallucinogenic drugs. Leary responded to the charges by arguing that LSD was not an "hallucinogenic" drug but rather a "psychedelic" drug.

What was Leary's point? His key argument was that a hallucinogenic drug was a drug that effected a distorted view of reality. Hallucinations involve delusions. But, claimed Leary, LSD effected not an illusory view of reality but a heightened ability to perceive reality. LSD was not mind-distorting, but mind-expanding. He cited the testimonies of numerous persons from the artistic world to buttress his claim. Artists told of being more acutely aware of color and texture while under the influence of the drug. Musicians claimed to be able to perceive previously unknown harmonics. People involved in the sexual revolution made claims that LSD so increased tactile sensitivity that users were able to experience orgasms in their elbows.

Who was able to refute these claims? The empirical, inductive method is haunted by the question of the limitations of our sensory organs and the question of how much the subject imposes on the data he is investigating.

PSYCHOLOGICAL PREJUDICES

This fourth category of causes for error looms as a constant threat to accurate conclusions. If a man's epistemological system is sound, his deductive reasoning impeccable, and his inductive procedure inerrant, all of this would still not guarantee proper conclusions. By reason of emotional bias he might still refuse to yield to the obvious conclusions of his research. A classic aphorism of our culture is "a man convinced against his will is of the same opinion still." This tendency to persevere in an opinion against all evidence is humorously illustrated by an anecdote related by the Lutheran theologian John Warwick Montgomery.

Once upon a time (note the mystical cast) there was a man who thought he was dead. His concerned wife and friends sent him to the friendly neighborhood psychiatrist. The psy-

chiatrist determined to cure him by convincing him of one fact that contradicted his belief that he was dead. The fact the psychiatrist decided to use was the simple truth that dead men do not bleed. He put his patient to work reading medical texts, observing autopsies, etc. After weeks of effort the patient finally said, "All right, all right! You've convinced me. Dead men do not bleed." Whereupon the psychiatrist stuck him in the arm with a needle, and the blood flowed. The man looked down with a contorted, ashen face and cried: "Good Lord! Dead men bleed after all!"[5]

Emotional prejudice is not limited to the dull-witted, the illiterate, and the poorly educated. It is exceedingly difficult for the most brilliant of men to be free of it. Philosophers and theologians are not free from vested interests and psychological prejudice that distort thinking.

The purpose of the foregoing survey of error factors is not to build a foundation for despair or provide a basis for resigned skepticism. Though the road to knowledge may be fraught with perils of error, it is a road that must be taken if we are to think at all. To be aware of the possibility of prejudice, or even of its clear existence, is not to cure it, but that awareness is a prerequisite for the cure.

The question of the existence of God is a question that provokes deep emotional and psychological prejudice. In the arena of theological-philosophical debate the stands are crowded with vested interests. It is precisely this dimension of psychological vested interest that has been the driving force for much speculation concerning the origin of religious belief.

NOTES
1. Wilhelm Windelband, *A History of Philosophy,* vol. 1 (New York: Harper & Row, 1958), 132.
2. Some interpreters of Anselm's classical ontological argument for the existence of God moved in this fashion. For a contemporary discussion of the problem, see John Hick and Arthur C. McGill, eds., *The Many-Faced Argument* (New York: Macmillan, 1967).

3. This narrow view of verification was propagated by the early school of Logical Positivism. For a broader evaluation of this method of verification, see Frederick Ferré, *Language, Logic and God* (New York: Harper & Row, 1961).
4. Irving M. Copi, *Introduction to Logic* (New York: Macmillan, 1953).
5. *The Altizer-Montgomery Dialogue* (Chicago: InterVarsity, 1967), 21.

CHAPTER 3
THE PSYCHOLOGY OF THEISM

Psychological prejudice may distort our reasoning, especially in regard to controversial issues. Perhaps there is no issue more vulnerable to bias than religion. We know that questions of religion touch virtually every aspect of our existence. Individuals' relationships to their families, their societies, and their cultures are often carried out in the midst of religious questions. The Orthodox Jew who marries a Christian feels the pressure of religious questions. The Roman Catholic who practices birth control feels the weight of ecclesiastical censure. Even the "liberated" prostitute discovers conflicts with her culture. Xaviera Hollander once confessed on a television talk show that despite all her claims to being a "Happy Hooker," she was unable to practice her trade if she found herself in a situation where church music was playing in the background. Even those who, like Hollander, would seem to have no connection whatever with religion still are affected by it. Why is this so? Why do even the most blatantly nonreligious people feel its influence on their lives? Is man incurably religious?

French scientist-philosopher Blaise Pascal touched the nerve of the issue in his classic definition of man as a paradox. Man finds himself suspended between the poles of infinity and nothingness, having the body of a beast and the mind of an angel. Man is acutely aware of his condition as he experiences the threat of nothingness. Man is caught in the paradox of being at the same time *homo grandeur* and *homo misere*. Man's grandeur lies in the ability to contemplate his own existence. But this grandeur is at the same time misery, for man can contemplate a better existence than he presently enjoys. Yet he is never able to actualize the possibilities he contemplates.[1]

It is precisely this ability to contemplate a better existence that lies behind most psychological theories for the origin of religion. The threat of our extinction or of nothingness provokes a wish for a future existence that is better than the one we now enjoy or endure. The notion of a heaven where there will be no death, no pain, no suffering, no tears, and no darkness can be enormously appealing to a miserable man. That undeniable appeal has been the rallying point for many opponents of religious belief.

SIGMUND FREUD'S ANALYSIS OF RELIGION

Freud was a convinced atheist as well as an astute observer of human beings. Like many other thinkers of the post-Enlightenment world, he wrestled with the question, If there is no God, why is there religion? Freud looked not to textbooks on religion but to the complexities of the human psyche for the answer to that question.

Freud pointed to the restrictions imposed on individuals by civilization as critical factors in the emergence of religion. In a society composed of individuals, restrictions on individual desires are necessary for mutual survival. Without societal restrictions, man is left in the brutal state of nature where only the strong—indeed, the strongest—can survive. In the face of the threat of nature, society is born. "The principle task of civilization, its actual raison d'etre, is to defend us against nature."[2] However, even civilization, no matter how well advanced, cannot totally vanquish the threat of nature.

*There are the elements, which seem to mock at all human
control: the earth, which quakes and is torn apart and
buries all human life and its works; water, which deluges
and drowns everything in a turmoil; storms, which blow
everything before them; there are diseases, which we have
only recently recognized as attacks by other organisms; and
finally there is the painful riddle of death, against which no
medicine has yet been found, nor probably will be. With
these forces nature rises up against us, majestic, cruel and
inexorable; she brings to our mind once more our weakness
and helplessness, which we thought to escape through the
work of civilization.*[3]

If civilization cannot control nature and remove its threat,
what can? The answer, of course, is the projection of religious
character on nature itself. Freud saw the first step as the hu-
manization of nature.

*Impersonal forces and destinies cannot be approached; they
remain eternally remote. But if the elements have passions
that rage as they do in our own souls, if death itself is not
something spontaneous but the violent act of an evil Will, if
everywhere in nature there are Beings around us of a kind
that we know in our own society, then we can breathe freely,
can feel at home in the uncanny and can deal by psychical
means with our senseless anxiety. We are still defenseless,
perhaps, but we are no longer helplessly paralyzed; we can
at least react.*[4]

Thus, once nature is humanized—personalized—the possibility of psychical reaction is insured. Persons can be dealt with
in a way impersonal forces cannot. If nothing else, persons
can be appeased or pleaded with. We learn how to deal with
hostile people in ways we cannot deal with tornadoes. We can
reason with, plead with, or bribe our human enemies. But
how does one negotiate with a flood or reason with cancer?
The answer is to make nature personal or to invest it with

personal deities who are willing and able to negotiate.

Freud traces the development of religion from a simple animism to a complex monotheism that culminated in belief in a benevolent Providence who manifests fatherlike characteristics. Once God becomes a single person, "man's relations to him could recover the intimacy and intensity of the child's relation to his father."[5]

The father image of God is also relevant to the origin of religion as it relates to the phenomenon of guilt. Both in *Totem and Taboo* and in *Civilization and Its Discontents,* Freud articulated his hypothesis of a primordial tribal struggle between the father-chief and the young sons, a struggle that culminated in the murder of the father. This deed left the young men with tormented consciences that were only relieved by the worship and appeasement of the now deified image of the departed father. Thus Freud presented a psychological basis for the phenomenon of religion. Fear of nature and guilt concerning the father comprise a two-sided basis for religious belief and practice.[6]

LUDWIG FEUERBACH'S ANALYSIS

Ludwig Feuerbach presented the nineteenth century with a critique of both religion in general and Christianity in particular. Feuerbach's basic thesis was that "Religion is the dream of the human mind."[7] He saw theology as being nothing more than anthropology. Man's deities, produced by a highly active imagination, are merely the projected images of himself. Religion, said Feuerbach, has its basis in the essential difference between man and brute—the brutes have no religion.

Man has religion because he has self-consciousness and the ability to think abstractly and project his abstractions to the ideal form. God is the projection of Absolute Personality. This God is important to man as He provides a means to reach the goal of immortality. Death is the catalyst for religion. If there was no death, there would be no religion. For Feuerbach, the resurrection of Christ was seen as "the realized wish of man to immediate certainty of his personal continuity of existence."[8] Feuerbach maintained that religion expresses the human attempt at apotheosis, deification.

Man's images of God are always anthropomorphic. That is, men create gods in man's own image. Our gods are mere mental projections of ourselves.

Such as are a man's thoughts and dispositions, such is his God; so much worth as a man has, so much and no more has his God. Consciousness of God is self-consciousness, knowledge of God is self-knowledge. By his God thou knowest the man, and by the man his God; the two are identical.[9]

Feuerbach went on to state that man's images of his gods vary from culture to culture and inevitably take on characteristics of the culture. The ancient Germans had a god who was a supreme warrior. The Homeric gods were dominated by Zeus because Zeus was the strongest of the gods, and physical strength was an exalted quality of the Homeric age. Caucasian cultures have white deities, negro cultures have black ones. Indian gods look and act like Indians and cowboy gods look and act like cowboys. Man's deities express his egoism. Feuerbach goes on to say, "If the plants had eyes, taste, and judgment, each plant would declare its own flower the most beautiful."[10] Thus, what man is not, but what he wills to be or wishes to be, just that and only that, nothing else, is God.

KARL MARX'S ANALYSIS
Marx was interested in the matter of religion not for metaphysical reasons but for reasons that related to his broader understanding of history. Picking up where Feuerbach left off, Marx claimed that religion has its roots in egoism and fantasy. Man seeks a superman who mirrors himself. Religion creates the fantasy that provides man with comfort, with an opium for the masses.

Marx saw the origin of religion as a peculiar manifestation of the class struggle. Religious doctrines are human fabrications invented by the ruling class for the purpose of economic exploitation. The poor worker is told by the "religious" ruler that poverty is a virtue. The gods are offered as the bearers of future bliss. The land beyond the grave is promised to the productive and obedient slaves. While the poor man looks for his future reward in heaven, the ruling class is getting rich at his present expense. The worker loses his material goods but keeps his soul intact for the future. Thus religion serves as a necessary tool to keep the workers from revolution.

In the conditions of the proletariat, those of old society at large are already virtually swamped. The proletarian is without property; his relation to his wife and children has no longer anything in common with the bourgeois family-relations; modern industrial labor, modern subjugation to capital, the same in England as in France, in America as in Germany, has stripped him of every trace of national character. Law, morality, religion are to him so many bourgeois prejudices, behind which lurk in ambush just as many bourgeois interests.[11]

So religion is due to the devious imagination of a particular segment of mankind. Religion is used by the bourgeois to protect themselves from a natural fear, the fear of a proletariat revolution.

FRIEDRICH NIETZSCHE'S ANALYSIS

Friedrich Nietzsche saw religion as having its roots in man's fear of facing the struggles of being locked in combat resulting from mutual lust for power. Religion provides a basis for morality which in turn keeps the potential "Superman" in check. In *Beyond Good and Evil*, Nietzsche distinguished between what he called a "slave morality" and a "master morality." The slave embraces a morality that exalts his own weakness, and the master espouses a morality that exalts his own power. In terms of slave, or "herd," morality, Nietzsche wrote,

Those qualities which serve to alleviate the existence of sufferers are brought into prominence and flooded with light; it is here that sympathy, the kind, helping hand, the warm heart, patience, diligence, humility, and friendliness attain to honor; for here these are the most useful qualities, and almost the only means of supporting the burden of existence. Slave morality is essentially the morality of utility. [12]

Nietzsche saw in Christianity the epitome of slave morality manifesting itself. He saw Christendom (particularly as it was manifested in nineteenth-century Europe) as the symbol of the complete destruction of natural values. Christianity is the negation and devaluation of all that is natural. It is the mortal enemy of natural ethics. Religions, particularly Christianity, were invented and perpetuated by weak men who could not face a universe where there are in fact no ultimate goals, no ultimate truths, no ultimate meaning. Religion signifies the victory of calm and restraint (symbolized by the Greek god Apollo) over raw power and energy (symbolized by the god Dionysus). It signifies the loss of man's heroic consciousness.

Behold, I teach you the Superman. The Superman is the meaning of the earth. Let your will say: the Superman shall be the meaning of the earth! I entreat you, my brothers, remain true to the earth, and do not believe those who speak to you of superterrestrial hopes! They are poisoners, whether they know it or not. [13]

Thus, according to Nietzsche, religion endures because weak men need it. He wrote concerning Christianity,

Most people in old Europe, as it seems to me, still need Christianity at present, and on that account it still finds

belief. For such is man: a theological dogma might be refuted to him a thousand times, provided, however, that he had need of it, he again and again accepts it as "true,"—according to the famous "proof of power" of which the Bible speaks.[14]

In these men—Freud, Feuerbach, Marx, and Nietzsche—we have some examples of great thinkers who have located the "whence" of religion in one aspect of man's psychological makeup or the other. Fear of nature, wish-projection, relief from guilt and anxiety, fear of economic revolution, and fear of nothingness are all labels for various psychological states that make religion appealing. To be left alone and unprotected in a hostile or indifferent universe is a terrifying thought. The proverbial maxim "necessity is the mother of invention" is applied to religion as well as to myriad drugs or television sets.

From a more contemporary perspective, English philosopher Bertrand Russell, who died in 1970, recapitulated the wish-projection motif as the answer to the question of the origin of religion. He wrote in his essay "Why I Am Not a Christian,"

Religion is based, I think, primarily and mainly upon fear. It is partly the terror of the unknown and partly, as I have said, the wish to feel that you have a kind of elder brother who will stand by you in all your troubles and disputes. Fear is the basis of the whole thing—fear of the mysterious, fear of defeat, fear of death. Fear is the parent of cruelty, and therefore it is no wonder if cruelty and religion have gone hand in hand. It is because fear is at the basis of those two things. In this world we can now begin a little to understand things, and a little to master them by help of science, which has forced its way step by step against the Christian religion, against the churches, and against the opposition of all the old precepts. Science can help us to get over this craven fear in which mankind has lived for so

*many generations. Science can teach us, and I think our
own hearts can teach us, no longer to look around for
imaginary supports, no longer to invent allies in the sky,
but rather to look to our own efforts here below to make this
world a fit place to live in, instead of the sort of place that
the churches in all these centuries have made it.*[15]

Any one of these psychological projections might possibly
explain the origin of religion. To prove that it does, however,
is a formidable task. The question of the origin of religion
cannot be settled ultimately by either the psychologist or the
philosopher. The question of the origin of religion is ultimately a question of history, not of psychology and philosophy. The psychologist may present us with data regarding
what the human psyche can and does like to project. He can
offer a multitude of possible psychological reasons why men
might invent religion. But to show what men can do and
might do is not to show what men actually do. To prove that
a man is capable of murder is insufficient evidence to convict
a man of murder. Though it is helpful to demonstrate that a
murder suspect had a motive for committing the crime, it
does not prove that he in fact committed the crime.

We must be careful to note that the above arguments can
never be used as proof for the nonexistence of God. They
can be useful for atheists who hear theists state that the only
possible explanation for religion is the existence of God. Such
an argument could be countered very nicely by the theories
mentioned in this chapter. There are, obviously, other explanations for the existence of religion.

In fact, all the arguments presented above really have no
bearing on the issue of the existence of God. Freud, Marx,
and the others were not attempting to disprove the existence
of God. Their arguments already presupposed the nonexistence of God. They were not dealing with the question, Is
there a God? They were dealing with the question, Since
there is no God, why is there religion? (If in fact there is no
God, their research is valuable to our understanding of man

and the phenomenon of religion.) The issue of theism/atheism is not over the question, Why does man believe in God? The ultimate issue is not why do men fear the problems of their existence, but rather *why are there thinking men in a universe worrying about the problems of existence?*

To show that men desire a God is not to demonstrate anything about whether or not there is, in fact, such a deity. Unless we can establish a principle to the effect that anything man desires to exist cannot or does not exist, the above explanations do not touch on the issue of the existence of God. These are psychological analyses that begin and end on the psychological level. They may teach us much concerning man, but say nothing with respect to God's existence. It is intriguing that many supposedly enlightened thinkers today base their unbelief or agnosticism on the above critiques, when, in fact, these critiques have no real bearing on the God question. The critiques have been repeated so many times that they have in effect hardened into orthodox dogma. (Thinkers who consider themselves liberal and open-minded often criticize Christians for holding to religious dogmas, yet unbelievers have dogma of their own, it seems.)

It is necessary to point out that classical theism does not rest its case for the existence of God on the phenomenon of religion. It is comforting to the theist that he is preserved from loneliness in the context of religion, but in terms of the debate, religion serves only as corroborative evidence for his faith, not compelling evidence for the existence of God. If the atheist could show that the only evidence for the existence of God that theists can offer is religious phenomena, then again a serious blow would be dealt to the theist.

It is also very important to note that what Freud and others offer are plausible alternate explanations to the origin of religion other than those offered by theists. It is one thing to demonstrate that man can fabricate religious experiences; it is another thing to demonstrate that he actually does so. It is one thing to argue that men can invent religion out of psychological necessity; it is another to argue that he does. The former involves questions of psychological and intellectual ability; the latter involves questions of history. When Freud spoke of origins, he was writing as a historian, not as a psychologist. We know his competence as a psychologist; his competence as a historian is certainly not so well attested.

There are, as we shall see, limitations in all the theories of these great thinkers.

FREUD'S LIMITATIONS

Freud has been very helpful to the intellectual world in showing that man has a dimension of religious desire. He has been even more helpful in relating the phenomenon of guilt to religious consciousness. Surely nature is threatening to man and produces anxiety and fear. Surely the threat of nature is indeed reduced by humanizing and personalizing it. Surely religion does offer a soothing comfort in light of that threat and stands as a highly desirable option. All of this may be true, but even if it is, we cannot then conclude that there is in fact no comforting reality such as God in the universe. I am not accusing Freud of drawing that conclusion, but countless thousands of people have drawn it and continue to do so. A benevolent Father may be an attractive incitement to religious devotion. On the other hand, an angry Father may be equally inciting to move toward atheism. Freud himself candidly admitted that an unpleasant experience he suffered in an encounter with his own father may have predisposed him toward feelings of antipathy to "Father-Gods."

FEUERBACH'S LIMITATIONS

Like Freud, Feuerbach contributed considerable insight into human religious phenomena. He called attention to the fact that men tend to portray their gods in their own image, giving to their deities characteristics and attributes of themselves. That men are prone to fashion religious idols in their own image is no surprise to the Christian. That human pride and arrogance manifest themselves in human religious practices and art should be carefully noted by every theist. But again, Feuerbach's analysis teaches us much about man, but precious little about the existence or nonexistence of God.

MARX'S LIMITATIONS

Marx's critique of religion has great value not only for the atheist but for the theist as well. At the point of demonstrating the use of religion to manipulate and exploit the poor and oppressed of this world, Marx has been prophetic. His insights into the dimensions of labor and economics are of lasting value. Since Marx, no one can afford to ignore the fact that man's labor has much to do with human history. Surely it is evident that religion has all too often served as an opium for the masses and a tool of exploitation for the rich. As insightful as Marx's critique of religion is, however, it adds nothing to the question of the existence of God. Most religions, especially Christianity, are quick to admit that religious institutions are given to exploitation and manipulation and a host of other evils. But the fact that man can invent a god for socioeconomic reasons is not to demonstrate that he has done so. Or if it can be shown that some or even most men "invent" a god for these reasons, it does not show that all men have.

NIETZSCHE'S LIMITATIONS

Friedrich Nietzsche seldom elicits ambivalent feelings in most theists. He was so fervently anti-Christian that it is hard for believers to discuss his life and work without boiling with rage. I for one am deeply impressed not only by his insights but by his passion. Like the Christian philosopher Søren Kierkegaard, Nietzsche offered a devastating critique of organized religion that I can deeply appreciate. His description of the decadence of European society, particularly at the moral level, is helpful. That heroic moral courage is all too often compromised or sacrificed to the security of the herd is undoubtedly true. If life is ultimately without value and man's basic characteristic is his lust for power, then Nietzsche has offered powerful reasons for negating not only God but religion as well. If the only reason people are religious is to escape the burden of exercising courage, then I would campaign for the end of religion. But again, these matters do not touch the issue of the existence of God, though they press heavily on the matter of religious behavior.

While valuable insights may be gained with respect to human behavior by an analysis of the role psychological desires play in religion, the question of the existence of God cannot be solved by these considerations. What is true can never be determined by an analysis of what men desire or do not desire to be the truth.

The fact remains, of course, that many people do indeed base their unbelief on the psychological arguments of Freud, Marx, and the others. In the following chapters we shall see that there are just as many arguments showing that unbelief has its roots in the psychological needs of man.

NOTES
 1. David E. Roberts, *Existentialism and Religious Belief* (New York: Oxford University Press, 1957).
 2. Sigmund Freud, *The Future of an Illusion*, trans. W. D. Robson-Scott (New York: Doubleday, 1964), 20.
 3. Ibid.
 4. Ibid., 22.
 5. Ibid., 27.
 6. See Sigmund Freud, *Civilization and Its Discontents*, trans. W. D. Robson-Scott (New York: Doubleday, 1964), 21ff.
 7. Ludwig Feuerbach, *The Essence of Christianity*, trans. George Eliot (New York: Harper & Row, 1957), xxxix.
 8. Ibid., 135.
 9. Ibid., 12.
10. Ibid., 8.
11. Karl Marx, *The Communist Manifesto* (Chicago: Gateway, 1954), 35.
12. See Robert N. Beck, ed., *Perspectives on Philosophy*, (New York: Holt, Rinehart & Winston, 1961), 370.
13. Friedrich Nietzsche, *Thus Spake Zarathustra*, trans. R. J. Hollingdale (Baltimore: Penguin, 1961), 42.
14. H. J. Blackham, ed., *Reality, Man and Existence: Essential Works of Existentialism* (New York: Bantam, 1965), 71.
15. Bertrand Russell, *Why I Am Not a Christian* (New York: Simon & Schuster, 1957), 22.

PART TWO

The Psychology of Unbelief

CHAPTER 4
THE FLIGHT FROM AN
INDIGNANT GOD

The views of Freud, Feuerbach, Marx, and Nietzsche have
been so widely disseminated in our culture that it is a common occurrence for the theist to have his faith challenged on
the basis of psychological charges. Is there any religious man
who has never been accused of believing in God merely because he needed a crutch to face the threats of the modern
world? That the shoe could be on the other foot or the
crutch used for the other leg is rarely considered.

In contrast to the widespread awareness of the psychology
of theism, there is a woeful ignorance of the psychology of
atheism. It is not common knowledge that the New Testament offers an answer to the question, If there is a God, why
is there atheism? The answer to the question is given in
what would now be called psychological categories. That is to
say, the New Testament maintains that unbelief is generated
not so much by intellectual causes as by moral and psychological ones. The problem is not that there is insufficient evidence to convince rational beings that there is a God, but
that rational beings have a natural hostility to the being of
God. In a word, the nature of God (at least the Christian

God) is repugnant to man and is not the focus of desire or wish-projection. Man's desire is not that the omnipotent, personal Judeo-Christian God exist, but that He not exist. The New Testament sees not only atheism but human-fabricated religion as being grounded in such antipathy toward the true God.

To gain a clear understanding of the charge leveled at natural man, it will be helpful to take a close look at the apostle Paul's letter to the Romans. In the first chapter of that letter, Paul gives an elaborate explanation of man's reaction to the knowledge of God.

For the wrath of God is revealed from heaven against all ungodliness and unrighteousness of men, who suppress the truth in unrighteousness. (Romans 1:18)

Paul begins by declaring the revelation of the wrath of God from heaven. This initial assertion is enough in itself to provoke a negative emotional reaction in many readers. The idea of the wrath of God is not a popular concept. The word Paul uses, which is translated by the English "wrath," is the Greek word *orge*. The wrath that Paul describes does not indicate an arbitrary, capricious, or irrational passion manifested in the Deity. Though God is indeed angry, His anger is directed against, and provoked by, the evil of men. Paul knows nothing of a divine blind fury that rages against innocent men. God's wrath is revealed against man's ungodliness and unrighteousness.

Ungodliness is a general term capable of various forms of particular content. The Greek term *asabea* means a general conduct of impiety and irreligiosity. Ungodliness involves a state of opposition to the majesty of God. Unrighteousness—*adikia*—indicates an assault against the righteousness of God. Many commentators interpret this passage as referring to two different kinds of human activity, namely, impiety and immorality. John Murray, for example, writes,

"Ungodliness" refers to perversity that is religious in char-
acter, "unrighteousness" to what is moral; the former is il-
lustrated by idolatry, the latter by immorality. The order is,
no doubt, significant. In the apostle's description of the de-
generacy, impiety is the precursor of immorality.[1]

Contrary to Murray, I adopt the position taken by Calvin
and, more recently, by Kittel's *Theological Dictionary of the
New Testament.*

A common view is that the reference is to sins against the
first and second tables of the Law, offenses against God and
neighbor. If so, it is natural to conclude, though there is no
exegetical support for this, that Paul has irreligion and im-
morality in view, and that the former is traced back to the
latter. Against this, however, is the pasan *which embraces*
both terms and binds them closely together. Another counter-
argument is that the distinction between sins against God
and against men is rare among the Rabbis and is certainly
not a Rabbinic distinction. A final point is that in what
follows adikia *covers both words. The* dike *against which men*
offend is God's righteousness. Hence asebeia *and* adikia *in*
Rom. 1:18 are a hendiadys: "ungodliness and unrighteous-
ness."[2]

The same general idea is expressed by the use of two
different nouns. God's wrath is directed against something
specific, which is considered to be an expression of both ungodliness and unrighteousness.

Paul does not leave us to speculate as to the particular evil
that is considered ungodly and unrighteous. He moves quickly
from the general to the specific and locates the particular
crime that provokes God. That crime is identified as wickedness that suppresses the truth. It is this suppression of the
truth that is at the heart of Paul's psychology of atheism.
Paul uses the expression *en adikia katechonton,* which has

been variously translated "holding (the truth) in unrighteousness," "hold down (the truth) in unrighteousness," "suppress (the truth)," "stifle," and "hinder." J. H. Bavinck has suggested another alternative to get at the matter, namely the word *repress*. He writes,

It seems to me that in this case we should translate it by "repress." We intentionally choose a word which has a specific meaning in psychological literature. Webster's Ninth New Collegiate Dictionary *defines the word* repression *as "a process by which unacceptable desires or impulses are excluded from consciousness and left to operate in the unconscious." This seems to agree with what Paul says here about human life. But we must mention that the word* repression *has received a wider meaning in more recent psychology. In Freudian psychology it specifically refers to unconscious desires of a more or less sexual nature. In more recent psychology it is also applied to desires and impulses of a very different nature. The impulses or desires which are repressed may be very valuable. Anything that goes contrary to the accepted patterns of life or to the predominant popular ideas may be repressed. Usually this happens, and the results can be far-reaching. We are reminded of this psychological phenomenon recently discovered by Paul's usage of the word. He says that man always naturally represses God's truth because it is contrary to his pattern of life.*[3]

The primary meaning of the verb *katakein* in biblical Greek is "to hold fast." In its most common usage it is a positive term such as "holding fast" to spiritual values, the word of God, etc. But the term is also used in a pejorative sense, meaning "holding illegally" or "holding in prison."[4] Paul, in Romans 1, is obviously using the term in a negative sense. Thus, man is said to hold the truth in an evil way. According to Bavinck it is a repressing or "holding down" of truth that ought not to be repressed or held down.

That which is known about God is evident within them; for God made it evident to them. (Romans 1:19)

Here the apostle asserts that knowledge of God is not a problem of obscurity that can be detected only by a intellectual elite group or by a skilled master of esoteric mysteries. That which can be known is plain. The word *plain* is the English translation of the Greek *phaneron*. (The Latin word is *manifestum*, from which our word *manifest* is derived.) This knowledge is not hidden or concealed, but manifest. It is clear and transparent for anyone to see. Paul goes on to say that the reason it is plain is because God shows it to them. In this case if the pupil doesn't learn, it is not because the teacher didn't teach. Not only is the knowledge plainly available, but the knowledge is made clear by God Himself.

Since the creation of the world His invisible attributes, His eternal power and divine nature, have been clearly seen, being understood through what has been made, so that they are without excuse. (Romans 1:20)

Much debate has arisen in the history of the church concerning the precise meaning of this verse. The debate centers around the controversy over whether God's revelation is mediate or immediate. That is, is the revelation gleaned by reasoning from the evidence of God in the creation, or is the revelation a kind of intuitive knowledge immediately impressed upon the consciousness of man? The question arises from a certain ambiguity in the Greek text. What does Paul mean when he says, "from the creation of the world"? Does this "from" *(apo)* mean a temporal period or a source of information? Most modern commentators favor the former and render the Greek "since" the creation of the world. Either translation is useful, however, for the point under consideration. Whatever the mode of revelation, the fact remains that God's invisible nature, even His power and deity, has been clearly perceived in the things that are made. Murray says:

And this sense of the term "clearly seen" is provided by the explanatory clause "being understood by the things that are made"—it is the seeing of understanding of intelligent conception. Stress is laid upon the perspicuity afforded by the things that are made in mediating to us the perception of the invisible attributes—they are "clearly seen."[5]

The things that are clearly seen are seen in the created things, namely nature. The cumulative effect of this knowledge that is clearly seen is to leave men "without excuse." Herein lies the basis of the universal guilt of man. No one can claim ignorance of the knowledge of God. No one can cite insufficient evidence for not believing in God. Though people are not persuaded by the evidence, this does not indicate an insufficiency in the evidence, but rather an insufficiency in man. This insufficiency is not a natural inability that provides man with an excuse. Man's failure to see this general and universal revelation of God is not because he lacks eyes or ears or a brain with which to think. The problem is not a lack of knowledge or a lack of natural cognitive equipment but a moral deficiency. Hence man is held to be at fault for his refusal to submit to the evidence God plainly provides. This critical distinction between the objective data and the subjective appropriation of it is one that is overlooked far too often. If man had no natural cognitive ability to receive the general revelation, God could hardly hold him responsible for it. But no such excuse can be claimed by man, as Paul emphatically states. Calvin says on this point:

But as the greater part of mankind, enslaved by error, walk blindfold in this glorious theater, he exclaims that it is a rare and singular wisdom to meditate carefully on these works of God, which many, who seem most sharp-sighted in other respects, behold without profit. It is indeed true, that the brightest manifestation of divine glory finds not one genuine spectator among a hundred. Still neither his power nor his wisdom is shrouded in darkness.[6]

To be sure, Calvin declares a kind of insufficiency of general revelation. It is insufficient to "lead us to the right path." That is, it is insufficient to convert us. He also speaks of a deficiency of the "natural powers" of man, but he is careful to point out that "as the dullness which prevents us is within, there is no room for excuse. We cannot plead ignorance, without being at the same time convicted by our own consciences both of sloth and ingratitude."[7] Elsewhere he comments, "We must, therefore, make this distinction, that the manifestation of God by which He makes His glory known among His creatures is sufficiently clear as far as its own light is concerned."[8]

Thus the lack of deficiency in general revelation is rooted not so much in man's natural composition as in his disposition. That is, the matter of the knowledge of God the Creator is not so much an intellectual problem as it is a moral problem. It becomes an intellectual problem because the mind is darkened by man's indisposition or psychological bias against the light. As Jesus said, "The light is come into the world, and men loved the darkness rather than the light; for their deeds were evil" (John 3:19). Paul reiterated this in the Letter to the Romans.

For even though they knew God, they did not honor Him as God, or give thanks; but they became futile in their speculations, and their foolish heart was darkened. (Romans 1:21)

Again Paul reaffirms that men "knew" God. The problem is not failure to honor what was not known, but a refusal to honor what was clearly known.

Paul not only asserts that revelation is provided and made available but asserts that the revelation penetrates man. (Here I must fault Calvin for his use of the "blindfold" image.) It is not as though God merely provides light and men refuse to look at it. The light gets through, as Calvin himself indicates. We not only have an external revelation, but we have a knowledge of that revelation. To argue that general revela-

tion fails to produce a "natural knowledge" of God is to do
serious violence to the text. Paul's complaint is not that men
failed to know God, but that they failed to honor Him. Herein
is the universal indictment of man.

Again, it is critical to repeat that the indictment is not rendered against men who are ignorant with or without just
cause. There can be no appeal to ignorance of the knowledge
of God. If there were no universal general revelation, an appeal could be lodged against God that His wrath was being
directed not only against people who knew nothing about
Him, but against people who had no possible way of knowing
anything about Him. That would be to hold people accountable for ignorance that could not be overcome. But the point
is that such a revelation is given so that invincible ignorance
cannot be the plea.

But what about ignorance that results from a refusal to
make use of the data made available to you? Can the atheist
plead that although the revelation was made available and
manifested clearly, objectively, and transparently, he didn't
"see" it because in his fear or pride or antipathy of any sort,
he refused to open his eyes to it? The answer must again be
in the negative, for Paul makes it clear that the light penetrates—knowledge is there. The judgment is not against
ignorance, but against the "holding of the truth" in unrighteousness. Knowledgeable men, not ignorant men, are the focal points of divine wrath and judgment.

In the use of "knowledge of God" in the New Testament,
there are clear indications that this knowledge (*gnosis*) can
be on different levels. The term is a pregnant one, filled with
various nuances. There is a difference between "knowing"
God theoretically and knowing Him personally, that is, in
terms of an intimate filial relationship. There is also the crucial difference between a knowledge of God and an acknowledgment of God which is precisely what the apostle is dealing
with here.[9] Men are judged for refusing to acknowledge what
they know to be true. No matter how many nuances or levels may be contained in the word (knowledge), there remains

the decisive distinction between knowledge *(gnosis)* and ignorance *(agnosia)*.

The apostle goes on to say that men who failed to honor
God or give thanks to Him (even while knowing Him) became futile in their thinking and their senseless hearts were
darkened. What follows from the refusal to acknowledge God
is the effect of futile reasoning. This reasoning is futile precisely because it proceeds from a primary premise that is
faulty and produces only the final fruit already present in the
initial bias. The end result is not light but darkness, which
penetrates to the very heart or core of man. It ends in darkness because it abhors the light at the beginning. Had the
reason first acknowledged the clear presence of the light, the
fatal process of reasoning would have never begun. Brilliant
and erudite reasoning may produce appalling conclusions if it
proceeds from a faulty starting point. A scientist who refuses
to acknowledge facts that he knows are true can hardly be
expected to arrive at sound conclusions. Any reasoning process that begins with a denial of the known and proceeds on
the basis of prejudice can hardly produce light, no matter
how lucid and cogent the argument may proceed after the
initial error is made.

It is important to note at this point that Paul does not
deny the ability of natural man to reason correctly. The problem is not in the capacity for thought per se, but in a
thought process that begins and is maintained by prejudice to
the facts. The intellectual problem is produced by the moral
problem, not the moral problem by an intellectual one.

*Professing to be wise, they became fools, and exchanged the
glory of the incorruptible God for an image in the form of
corruptible man and of birds and four-footed animals and
crawling creatures. (Romans 1:22-23)*

This severe indictment by the apostle could easily be mis-
construed as an assault upon the intelligence of natural man.
A close look, however, shows that this passage attacks not

the intellectual ability of men but man's morality. Paul's use of
the term *fools* must be examined closely.

In biblical categories the term fool does not necessarily indicate a person of low intelligence. The term carries both a
moral and religious judgment. To be sure, the word is capable
of being used to describe persons who are dull-witted or have
an extraordinarily low degree of common sense. The Greek
word *moros* is the root from which the English "moron" derives. In classical Greek the term had a psychological flavor.
Bertram points out:

*With reference to men the use is predominantly psychologi-
cal. The word implies censure on man himself: his acts,
thoughts, counsels, and words are not as they should be. The
weakness may be due to a specific failure in judgment or
decision, but a general deficiency of intellectual and spiritual capacities may also be asserted.*[10]

In Old Testament terms the fool stands in sharp contrast
to the wise man. The wise man is known not by his academic credentials but by his practical manifestation of godliness. Wisdom begins with the "fear of the Lord." Conversely,
foolishness has its origin in the rejection of God. It is the fool
who says in his heart there is no God (Psalm 14:1). Isaiah
calls the man a fool who contemptuously breaks off fellowship
with God and becomes a practical atheist. To be a fool is to
fall into a negative theological category rather than an exclusively intellectual one. Likewise, the fool of the New Testament is the one who fails to act prudently with respect to
God, falling under moral judgment.

Paul's critique in this text is a two-edged sword. Not only
is the natural man labeled a fool, but he is pronounced guilty
of hypocrisy as well. The one who becomes a fool is the
same one who professes to be wise. There is a serious dis-
crepancy between a profession of wisdom and the reality of
wisdom. The man's guilt is compounded by the fact that
while being a fool he proclaims that he is wise. He claims a

state he doesn't have and thus falls under the double indictment of the apostle.

The foolishness of man is manifested in the exchanging of
the glory of God for idols. The word *exchange* is important
to a proper understanding of the text. Many translations often render the verb as "change." But the total context of the
passage excludes this rendition as it is too weak and ambiguous. A particular kind of change is in view here; one that
involves a mutation or a distortion that involves a kind of
substitution of one thing for another. This substitution involves the replacing of the genuine with the counterfeit. (The
physiological ramifications of this exchange will be explored
later.) The change results in idolatry, which also comes under
the judgment of God. Here is a case where the distortion of
truth results not in militant atheism but in a kind of religion.
This religion, however, does not serve to exonerate man or
mitigate the wrath of God, but rather compounds the felony
as it adds massive insult to the glory of the immortal God.
Pagan religion is not viewed as a step of evolutionary progress on the way to a fully developed monotheism, but a step
on the pathway of flight and retreat from monotheism. Not
evolution but devolution or even revolution (in the sense of
revolt against God) is the pattern of pagan religion. Murray
adds:

*Here the apostle sets forth the origin of that degeneration
and degradation which pagan idolatry epitomizes, and we
have the biblical philosophy of false religion. "For heathen-
ism," as Meyer says, "is not the primeval religion, from
which man might gradually have risen to the knowledge of
the true God, but is, on the contrary, the result of a falling
away from the known original revelation of the true God in
His works."*[11]

Historian of religion Mircea Eliade writes about the notion
of a "remote God" that is found widely in primitive religions.
He says,

*Celestially structured supreme beings tend to disappear
from the practice of religion, from cult; they depart from
among men, withdraw to the sky, and become remote, inac-
tive gods (dei otiosi). In short, it may be said of these gods
that, after creating the cosmos, life, and man, they feel a
sort of fatigue, as if the immense enterprise of the creation
had exhausted their resources. So they withdraw to the sky,
leaving a son or a demiurge on earth to finish or perfect
the Creation. Gradually their place is taken by other divine
figures—the mythical ancestors, the mother-goddesses, the fe-
cundating gods, and the like.*[12]

Eliade goes on to say that among African peoples, "The
great celestial god, the supreme being, all-powerful creator,
plays only a minor role in the religious life of most tribes. He
is too far away or too good to need an actual cult, and he is
involved only in extreme cases."[13]

Thus, even in primitive religion there is at least a vague
recollection of God the Creator. According to Paul, religion is
not the fruit of a zealous pursuit of God, but the result of a
passionate flight from God. The glory of God is exchanged
for an idol. The idol stands as a monument, not to religious
fervor but to the flight of man from his initial encounter with
the glory of God.

*Therefore God gave them over in the lusts of their hearts to
impurity, that their bodies might be dishonored among
them. For they exchanged the truth of God for a lie, and
worshiped and served the creature rather than the Creator,
who is blessed forever. Amen. (Romans 1:24-25)*

The response of God to the work of idolatry is seen in a
kind of divine abandonment of men. God lets man pursue his
lusts or desires for impurity. The working out of this abandoned lust culminates in the dishonoring of the human. What
begins as an act of refusal to honor God ends in the dishonoring of men. Karl Barth comments, "When God has been de-

prived of His glory, men are also deprived of theirs. Desecrated within their souls, they are desecrated also without in their bodies, for men are one."[14]

Paul's analysis indicates a progression not only from God to man but also from thought to deed. As behavior and theory are distinguishable, yet inseparably related, the moral consequences of the rejection of the knowledge of God will be inevitably manifested in moral conduct. Luther adds

Hence, also, the guilt is greater, for the aberration of idolatry and of an empty knowledge of God is now sealed not merely in the mind but in deed and action, thus becoming an example and a stumbling block that leads others into temptation. When, within the limits of their reverence for His holy name, they disgrace God in their thoughts by conceiving of Him in a fashion that is more than unworthy of Him, it is only right that they should fall back upon their heads, and that they should think and correspondingly act in a way that is unworthy of their humanity.[15]

Paul again makes reference to an "exchange" that is involved in idolatry. The exchange involves the substitution of a lie in place of the truth of God. This is the essence of idolatry, namely the worshiping of the created realm in place of, or instead of, the Creator. In the practice of idolatrous religion the intrinsic antithesis between truth and falsehood is obscured. That the pagan is "religious" in no way lessens his guilt before God. The practice of idolatrous religion is not viewed as an approximate form of authentic religion but as a negation of it. It is one thing to deny the existence of God; it is another thing to add insult to the denial by worshiping something that is clearly of the created order. The worship and service rendered to idols may be sincere, yet it is regarded as being sincerely evil. A sincere distortion of the truth that dishonors God evokes nothing less than the sincere wrath of God. As Paul elsewhere indicates in his reaction to the Greeks at Mars' Hill in Athens, God is not particularly pleased or flattered by altars inscribed with the legend, TO THE UNKNOWN GOD. Such worship is declared as being grounded in superstition rather than reality.

For this reason God gave them over to degrading passions; for their women exchanged the natural function for that which is unnatural, and in the same way also the men abandoned the natural function of the woman and burned in their desire toward one another, men with men committing indecent acts and receiving in their own persons the due penalty of their error. (Romans 1:26-27)

Again the apostle speaks of God's "giving them up." God removes the restraints from those who flee from Him and allows them to follow the course of their own drives. Their dishonorable degeneracy is in no way limited to homosexual practices but is made particularly manifest by that activity. It is not strange that Paul should appeal to homosexuality as an indication of radical degeneracy in light of the Old Testament view of it. Under the Mosaic Law homosexuality was regarded as an abomination to God and was a capital crime. It was also viewed as a serious enough sin to defile the land, a type of sin that was considered part of the customary practices of pagan nations with which Israel was forbidden to consort. (See Leviticus 18:22-30; 20:13.)

And just as they did not see fit to acknowledge God any longer, God gave them over to a depraved mind, to do those things which are not proper. (Romans 1:28)

The giving up to a base mind and improper conduct is not an arbitrary action of God. There is a reason for this punitive measure. The reason is clear: "they did not see fit to acknowledge God." The judgment of man upon God was the judgment that God was not worthy of human consideration. The error of the human mind does not proceed from a mere

logical miscalculation. It was not an error flowing out of logical reasoning, but a deliberate evaluation of the worth of the
knowledge of God. The error of the pagan is not accidental,
but clearly deliberate. The "not seeing fit" is an obstinate refusal to acknowledge that which is manifestly true.

*[They are] filled with all unrighteousness, wickedness,
greed, evil; full of envy, murder, strife, deceit, malice; they
are gossips, slanderers, haters of God, insolent, arrogant,
boastful, inventors of evil, disobedient to parents, without
understanding, untrustworthy, unloving, unmerciful; and
although they know the ordinance of God, that those who
practice such things are worthy of death, they not only do
the same, but give hearty approval to those who practice
them. (Romans 1:29-32)*

This catalogue of crimes arising out of an initial rejection
of the knowledge of God is ghastly. This list of human violations of divine law does not indicate that man's problem of
psychological prejudice toward God is a mild one. Indeed, the
hostility is deep and reflects not a minor disinclination, but a
burning rage in the very heart of man.

Another element is added to the content of the knowledge
of God revealed in creation. Not only is God's existence
known, but His attitude toward evil is likewise made manifest. (Paul develops this moral aspect of general revelation in
the second chapter of Romans.) The pagan knows the penalty for his evil. The astonishing dimension of the pagan's madness, however, is seen not only in that he blatantly practices
what he knows to be evil, and knows will be punished, but he
applauds and encourages others to participate in his madness
with him. Murray remarks

*To put it bluntly, we are not only bent on damning our-
selves but we congratulate others in the doing of those
things that we know have their issue in damnation. We
hate others as we hate ourselves and render therefore to*

them the approval of what we know merits damnation. Iniquity is most aggravated when it meets with no inhibition from the disapproval of others and when there is collective, undissenting approbation.[16]

The foregoing conclusion with respect to the immoral character of human behavior sets in bold relief the utter folly of it. This description of human endeavor manifests a kind of mass insanity. Insane not in the sense of behavior that is radically abnormal or atypical, but rather a kind of "normal" madness which is the inevitable result of an irrational process. Sin in the lives of rational beings begins on an irrational foundation: the refusal to acknowledge as true what one knows with clarity to be true.

The list of evils Paul enumerates are not to be found exclusively in the confines of special isolated groups of a particularly degenerate of primitive society. Paul is not describing the savage behavior of some remote tribe of headhunting cannibals or the moral pattern of the most calloused men in a maximum security prison. Where on earth could we go to find a man free from covetousness? Where could we go in pursuit of a man without envy? What society includes human beings free from insolence, boastfulness, and haughtiness? No, the evils elucidated are "normal" and "typical" of men everywhere. They are manifestations of the normal irrationalism of the most sophisticated society. Why? Why does rational man behave in such an irrational manner? Can we explain this by appealing to a subliminal sex drive? Have we answered the question adequately by simply appealing to Nietzsche's "lust for power"? From whence comes this "lust for power"?

THE PSYCHOLOGY OF ROMANS 1

To translate Paul's analysis of man's response to the knowledge of God into contemporary categories of psychology is not a difficult task, as indicated earlier by Bavinck's analysis. The basic stages of man's reaction to God can be formulated by means of the categories of trauma, repression, and substitution.

TRAUMA

Trauma may be defined as "an injury (as a wound) to living tissue caused by an extrinsic agent" and "a disordered psychic or behavioral state resulting from mental or emotional stress or physical injury."[17] So trauma can refer to mental and emotional shock as well as physical. A traumatic experience generally involves something negative or threatening to the individual. (Though it is also recognized that a positive surprise can be shocking in a traumatic way.) In the case of Paul's analysis the trauma is produced by man's encounter with God's self-revelation. Confrontation with God shocks and injures man. For various reasons, which will be explored in depth in later chapters, God's presence is severely threatening to man. God manifests a threat to man's moral standards, a threat to his quest for autonomy, and a threat to his desire for concealment. God's revelation involves the intrusion and indeed invasion of the "other," the "different," the alien and strange to human circumstances. In a word, it represents the invasion of light into the darkness to which men are accustomed.

On a physical plane we are aware of the painful results produced when we emerge from a situation of prolonged darkness into the blazing brightness of sunlight. Coal miners must be careful to adjust their eyes gradually as they emerge from their subterranean labors into daylight. Even those who walk above ground in the midst of daylight must be careful not to gaze directly into the sun lest they cause traumatic damage to their eyes. Calvin notes,

If, at midday, we either look down to the ground, or on surrounding objects which lie open to our view, we think ourselves endued with a very strong and piercing eyesight; but when we look up to the sun, and gaze at it unveiled, the sight which did excellently well for the earth, is instantly so

dazzled and confounded by the refulgence, as to oblige us to confess that our acuteness in discerning terrestrial objects is mere dimness when applied to the sun. Thus, too, it happens in estimating our spiritual qualities. So long as we do not look beyond the earth, we are quite pleased with our own righteousness, wisdom, and virtue; we address ourselves in the most flattering terms, and seem only less than demigods. But should we once begin to raise our thoughts to God, and reflect what kind of Being he is, and how absolute the perfection of that righteousness, and wisdom, and virtue, to which, as a standard, we are bound to be conformed, what formerly delighted us by its false show of righteousness, will become polluted with the greatest iniquity; what strangely imposed upon us under the name of wisdom, will disgust by its extreme folly; and what presented the appearance of virtuous energy, will be condemned as the most miserable impotence. So far are those qualities in us, which seem most perfect, from corresponding to the divine purity.[18]

So an encounter with the light of God's revelation is a traumatic experience for man. There is no trauma if the eyes are forever closed so that no light penetrates. But the eyes close in reaction to the shock of the light—after the pain has been experienced.

REPRESSION

Repress may be defined as follows: "To check by or as if by pressure; curb; to put down by force; subdue; . . . to prevent the natural or normal expression, activity, or development of; to exclude from consciousness."[19]

In the case of God's revelation, man encounters something ominously threatening that is traumatic. The memory of conscious knowledge of the trauma is not maintained in its clear, threatening state but is repressed. It is "put down" or "held in captivity" in the unconsciousness. But that which is repressed is not destroyed. The memory remains, though it may be buried in the unconscious realm. Knowledge of God is unacceptable to man, and as a result man does his best to blot it out or at least camouflage it in such a way that its threatening character can be concealed or dulled. That the human psyche is capable of such repression has been thoroughly demonstrated in a multitude of ways. The critical factor, however, for our discussion, is that the knowledge is not obliterated or destroyed. It remains intact but deeply submerged.

SUBSTITUTION

It is because repressed knowledge is not destroyed that substitution or "exchange" *(metallaso)* takes place. Again Bavinck comments,

This phenomenon of replacing, of substituting, is so common that we see it everywhere. It has been discovered that these repressed impulses of which we spoke, which "are left to operate in the unconsciousness," are not dead. They remain strong, and try to reassert themselves again and again. Surely, they play no part in man's conscious life, but they succeed in showing every now and again that they still exist. This has been illustrated by the story of the boy sent out of class at school who kept throwing stones against the windows of the school to show that he was still there. Freud particularly has called attention to this phenomenon and inaugurated its study. He noticed that the impulses which have been exiled to the unconscious may very well reveal themselves in the errors we make, in our slips of the tongue. But they especially crop up in dreams, for then they get the chance to come to the surface.[20]

In the substitution-exchange process, the repressed knowledge manifests itself outwardly in a veiled form. The original knowledge is threatening; its disguised form is much less threatening. When dealing with deep-rooted anxieties of uncertain origin, psychologists and psychiatrists frequently explore, with meticulous care, what may be termed the symbolic activity of mankind. Dreams, Freudian slips, bodily gestures, etc., all are involved in the careful scrutiny of the scientist seeking to unravel the complexities of the human psyche. For example, if in the course of a counseling interview, a person exhibits an involuntary twitch or tic every time he mentions his mother, the counselor will consider that significant. He will probe further into the area of the person's past relationship with his mother, even though the person may protest and give every assurance that there are no problems in that area of his life. In a word, what cannot be squarely and comfortably faced in the conscious mind may be borne with a relative degree of comfort at the unconscious level.

In theological terms, what results from the repression is the profession of atheism, either in militant terms or in its less militant form of agnosticism, or in a kind of religion that makes God less of a threat than he really is. Either option, atheism or diluted religion, manifests an exchange of the truth for a lie. The truth is exchanged for the lie simply because the lie seems easier to live with.

The judgment of the New Testament is that religion is, in many cases, man-made. Karl Barth pointed out that even Christianity can and often does become such a religion. This religion expresses not the fruit of man's pursuit of God, but the product of his substitution-exchange propensity. Bavinck goes on to say with respect to religion,

Thus, all kinds of ideas of God are formed; the human mind as the fabrica idolorum *(Calvin) makes its own ideas of God and its own myths. This is not intentional deceit— it happens without man's knowing it. He cannot get rid of them. So he has religion; he is busy with a god; he serves his god—but he does not see that the god he serves is not God Himself. An exchange has taken place—a perilous exchange. An essential quality of God has been blurred because it did not fit in with the human pattern of life, and the image man has of God is no longer true. Divine revela-*

tion indeed lies at the root of it, but man's thoughts and aspirations cannot receive it and adapt themselves to it. In the image man has of God we can recognize the image of man himself.[21]

The idea that man is capable of and has a proclivity for the manufacture of religion is not unique with Freud, Feuerbach, or Marx. Calvin pointed out in the sixteenth century, appealing to sources originating centuries earlier. That human religion reveals much of man's desires is clearly obvious. But it must be insisted that at least the biblical God manifests characteristics and features that are less than desirable for most men. With the numerous references to His expressions of wrath and judgment, His absolute claim over human life, etc., is it any surprise that His appearance is traumatic?

The Christian church has had to struggle in every generation against those who would lessen the traumatic dimension of God by substitution and distortion. The twentieth century is no exception. We have witnessed massive attempts to soften the demands imposed upon us by the biblical God. Consider, for example, the Bultmannian school, which seeks to demythologize the Scriptures and produces a theology that disregards the threatening character of history. An analysis of this antihistorical and anti-intellectual approach to theology raises the question as to whether the real mythology is in the New Testament or in the reconstructed Christianity the Bultmannian school represents. It is equally interesting to see the end result of Paul Tillich's teaching about the "God-beyond-God," or "ultimate concern." In spite of Tillich's literal apoplexy over the claims of his followers, he was the motivating force behind the proclamation of the death of God and the rise of "Christian atheism."

A strange irony attaches itself to much of contemporary theology. The "hard sayings" of Jesus are removed from the danger zone of encounter, the motifs of transcendence and "otherness" are rendered safe by demythologizing, and Jesus Himself is reduced to the realm of the "historically conditioned." Gollwitzer raises the obvious question, "Why should anyone attach unconditional importance to that which is conditioned?"[22] That question sounds strangely like the kind of question the prophets of Israel raised to those who fashioned idols out of wood and stone and then proceeded to bow down and worship the work of their own hands. While it is intimidating to bow down in awe before the powerful God of the Bible, it it utterly pointless to bow politely to false gods of our own making.

NOTES
1. John Murray, *The Epistle to the Romans,* vol. 1 of *The New International Commentary on the New Testament* (Grand Rapids: Eerdmans, 1959), 36.
2. Werner Foerster, *"asebes,"* vol. 7 of the *Theological Dictionary of the New Testament,* ed. Gerhard Kittel and Gerhard Friedrich, trans. Geoffrey W. Bromiley (Grand Rapids: Eerdmans, 1971), 190 (hereafter cited as *TDNT*).
3. J. H. Bavinck, *The Church Between the Temple and Mosque* (Grand Rapids: Eerdmans, n.d.), 118-119.
4. Herman Hanse, *"katecho,"* vol. 2 of the *TDNT,* 829.
5. Murray, *Epistle to the Romans,* 38-39.
6. John Calvin, *Institutes of the Christian Religion,* vol. 1, trans. Henry Beveridge (Grand Rapids: Eerdmans, 1964), 57.
7. Ibid., 62.
8. David W. Torrance and Thomas F. Torrance, eds., *The Epistles of Paul the Apostle to the Romans and to the Thessalonians,* vol. 8 of *Calvin's Commentaries,* trans. Ross MacKenzie (Grand Rapids: Eerdmans, 1961), 31.
9. Rudolf Bultmann writes, "Thus in the concept of the knowledge of God the element of knowledge emerges alongside and sometimes prior to that of acknowledgment. The two are obviously linked in Rom. 1:18-23 (esp. 21)" *("aion,"* vol. 1 of the *TDNT,* 205).
10. George Bertram, *"moros,"* vol. 4 of the *TDNT,* 832.
11. Murray, *Epistle to the Romans,* 41.
12. Mircea Eliade, *The Sacred and Profane,* trans. William R. Trask (New York: Harper & Row, 1957), 122-123.
13. Ibid.
14. Karl Barth, *The Epistle to the Romans,* 6th ed., trans. Edwyn C. Hoskyns (London: Oxford University Press, 1933).
15. Wilhelm Pauck, ed., *Luther: Lectures on Romans,* vol. 15 of *The Library of Christian Classics,* ed. John Baillie, John T. McNeill, and Henry P. Van Dusen (Philadelphia: Westminster, 1961), 33.
16. Murray, *Epistle to the Romans,* 53.
17. *Webster's Ninth,* s.v. "trauma."
18. Calvin, *Institutes,* 1:38-39.
19. *Webster's Ninth,* s.v. "repress."
20. Bavinck, *Between Temple and Mosque,* 121.
21. Ibid., 122.
22. Helmut Gollwitzer, *The Existence of God as Confessed by Faith,* trans. James W. Leith (Philadelphia: Westminster, 1965), 89ff.

CHAPTER 5
THE TRAUMA OF HOLINESS

In the last chapter we looked at the psychology of denying the existence of an almighty Being. Now we will consider an aspect of that Being, an aspect which is little understood by contemporary man but which is still important in the flight from belief. That aspect is holiness.

In 1910 a book was published in Germany under the simple title *Das Heilige (The Holy)*. In this short work theologian Rudolf Otto paved the way for a new evaluation of religious experience. Otto's work, which appeared under the English title *The Idea of the Holy*, was unique in its approach. Instead of examining the ideas found in various religions of the world, Otto studied the phenomenon of human reaction to the experience of the holy. Noted historian of religion Mircea Eliade says of Otto,

Gifted with great psychological subtlety, and thoroughly prepared by his twofold training as theologian and historian of religions, he succeeded in determining the content and specific characteristics of religious experience. Passing over the rational and speculative side of religion, he concentrated chiefly on its irrational aspect.[1]

Though Otto sought to explore and analyze the "irrational" or "nonrational" dimension of religion from a natural perspective, he was in no way seeking to instruct or enhance an irrationalism or subjectivism in theology. He says in the foreword of the English edition,

I do not thereby want to promote in any way the tendency of our time towards an extravagant and fantastic "irrationalism," but rather to join issue with it in its morbid form. The "irrational" is today a favorite theme of all who are too lazy to think or too ready to evade the arduous duty of clarifying their ideas and grounding their convictions on a basis of coherent thought.[2]

Typically, we tend to think that something that is holy is something good, something pure. In his analysis of the word *holy,* Otto points out that, though the moral quality of goodness is present in the term, it cannot be exhausted by it or equated with it. Though holiness contains the notion of absolute goodness, there remains a certain "extra," an "overplus." This "overplus" is defined by Otto as the "numinous."

I shall speak, then, of a unique "numinous" category of value and of a definitely "numinous" state of mind, which is always found wherever the category is applied. This mental state is perfectly sui generis *and irreducible to any other; and therefore, like every absolutely primary and elementary datum, while it admits of being discussed, it cannot be strictly defined.[3]*

The experience of the numinous provides what Otto calls "creature-feeling."[4] This feeling involves a band of feeling of dependence that is "a first subjective concomitant and effect of another feeling-element, which casts it like a shadow, but which in itself indubitably has immediate and primary reference to an object outside the self."[5] That is, the feeling of

creatureliness is a subjective response to the objective numinous.

The feeling of terror is basic to the experience of what is
holy and sacred. In further analysis, Otto adopts the term
mysterium tremendum to capture the experience of the
Holy.

MYSTERIUM TREMENDUM

Otto analyzes the notion of *tremendum* by isolating its con-
stituent elements. First is the element of awfulness—not awful in the sense of being bad but in the literal sense of being
"full of awe." This awfulness is of a peculiar nature. The emo-
tion of fear is closely connected with it, but it is not quite the
same. We derive words like *tremor* and tremble from the
concept of *tremendum.* The fear associated with the element
of awfulness is one that produces tremors or trembling. We
think of Søren Kierkegaard's words about Abraham in his
Fear and Trembling, in which he scrutinized the peculiar
kind of "awful dread that is experienced in the presence of
God." Or we think of the black spiritual "Were You There
When They Crucified My Lord?" with its ominous refrain,
"Sometimes it causes me to tremble, tremble, tremble."

Otto notes the close relationship between the awfulness
element and the Greek term *sebastos.* This title in its Latin
form is *augustus.* He notes the early Christian antipathy to
the use of the title *augustus* with reference to any man,
even the emperor. "They felt that to call a man *sebastos* was
to give a human being a name proper only to the numen, to
rank him by the category proper only to the numen, and that
it therefore amounted to a kind of idolatry."[6]

This awe is a sort of reverent fear that produces a shud-
dering kind of dread. The development of the usage of the
term awful suggests that there is a strong negative feeling
associated with the experience of religious awe. The term
awful is now used almost exclusively as a synonym for bad
or very bad.

The second element of the *tremendum* is the element of "overpoweringness." Otto links this awareness of might and power with the Latin *majestas*. Confrontation with this majestic power evokes a sense of impotence, inadequacy, and general nothingness. A biblical example of this dimension of encounter with the Holy may be seen in the case of Job.

After the narrative relating Job's experience with miserable afflictions, softened not at all by the judgmental counsel of his friends or the earthy pragmatism of his wife, we read of Job's plea for an answer to his condition from God.

Oh, that I had one to hear me! Behold, here is my signature; let the Almighty answer me! (Job 31:35)

In this plea, Job addresses God as the "Almighty." The particular title he uses is the Hebrew *El Shaddai*. This name for God appears more frequently in the Book of Job (thirty times) than in any other book of the Old Testament. The name dates from patriarchal times and connotes strongly the awesome power of God. Various translations of *El Shaddai* include "the Destroyer," "the All-Powerful One" and "the Overpowerer."[7]

Following the discourse of Elihu, God responds to Job in terms of an overpowering interrogation. God begins the interrogation with a devastating question that at the same time pronounces a judgment on Job.

Who is this that darkens counsel by words without knowledge? Now gird up your loins like a man, and I will ask you, and you instruct Me! (Job 38:2-3)

What follows is a lengthy series of questions that leave Job in a state of near collapse.

Where were you when I laid the foundations of the earth? Who laid its cornerstone? . . . Have the gates of death been revealed to you? . . . Can you bind the chains of the Ple-

*iades; or loose the cords of Orion? . . . Do you know the time
the mountain goats give birth? Do you observe the calving of
the deer? . . . Is it by your understanding that the hawk
soars, stretching his wings toward the south? (Job 38–39)*

And so the interrogation proceeds until God brings it to a
halt by a direct question of Job.

*Will the faultfinder contend with the Almighty? Let him
who reproves God answer it. (Job 40:1- 2)*

Notice Job's reaction. He cries out,

*Behold, I am insignificant; what can I reply to Thee? I lay
my hand on my mouth. Once I have spoken, and I will not
answer; even twice, and I will add no more. (Job 40:3-5)*

Job's reaction is a classic response of a sense of insignificance and impotence when confronted by the "overpoweringness" of the Holy.

A similar episode indicated by the prophet Jeremiah manifests the same kind of human response to the "overpoweringness" of God. He cries out to God,

*O LORD, Thou hast deceived me and I was deceived; Thou
hast overcome me and prevailed. (Jeremiah 20:7)*

Here Jeremiah experiences being "overwhelmed" by God.
Again Eliade says,

*He finds the feeling of terror before the sacred, before the
awe-inspiring mystery* (mysterium tremendum), *the majesty*
(majestas) *that emanates an overwhelming superiority of
power.*[8]

There is a sense in which confrontation with absolute
power produces a sense of absolute intimidation.

The third element of the *tremendum* isolated by Otto is the element of "energy" or urgency. This has to do with the features of the numinous object. Otto says,

It is particularly vividly perceptible in the orge *or "wrath"; and it everywhere clothes itself in symbolical expressions— vitality, passion, emotional temper, will, force, movement, excitement, activity, impetus.*[9]

In the human experience of the Holy, the Holy is not encountered in a lethargic state. The Holy is not experienced as "Being-in-Inertia" or as a neutral idea. There is something dynamic and moving in the encounter. The Holy thing is perceived as something that can *act*. This dynamic element, whether it be wrath or love, is in part responsible for the human reaction. The reaction is not to a static reality, but to an active one. Thus the Holy is encountered not as a sleeping giant who can be safely avoided by careful circumnavigation but as one whose dynamism is overwhelming.

THE MYSTERIUM

That mankind finds something "mysterious" about the Holy is not surprising. In the age of radio in the forties one of the most popular mystery programs was "Inner Sanctum." Part of the suspenseful intrigue of the program was its opening theme—the eerie, spine-tingling sound of a door creaking open as the announcer ominously said, "Inner Sanctum. . . ." Literally, the name of the program meant "in the holy." Even in this popular mode of communication a link was seen between the holy and the mysterious.

According to Otto, the *mysterium* is closely linked to the "otherness" of the Holy. The strangeness and unknown dimension of the Holy adds to the spirit of fear that attends encounter with it. Though terrifying, the Holy, the "Other" is also fascinating. There is the strange mixture of daunting awefulness with something uniquely attractive and fascinating. Otto says,

These two qualities, the daunting and the fascinating, now combine in a strange harmony of contrasts, and the resultant dual character of the numinous consciousness, to which the entire religious development bears witness, at any rate from the level of the "daemonic dread" onwards, is at once the strangest and most noteworthy phenomenon in the whole history of religion. (In Latin, daemon *did not originally mean a demon or evil spirit. It simply referred to any spirit or divine being.) The daemonic-divine object may appear to the mind as an object of horror and dread, but at the same time it is no less something that allures with a potent charm, and the creature, who trembles before it, utterly cowed and cast down, has always at the same time the impulse to turn to it, nay, even to make it somehow his own.*[10]

A child's fascination with ghost stories is a typical manifestation of the peculiar combination of fear and fascination. Children beg to hear such tales and yet often fail to endure the telling of them. My own son, when he was seven years old, begged me for permission to sleep out in the forest on a nearby mountain with a visiting college student. He thought it would be a spooky experience that would also be fun. The adventure began with unspeakable derring-do and gusto. However, after the campfire died and the conversation in the tent ceased, my junior explorer was left in the darkness with his attention riveted to those "things that go bump in the night." He said nothing for thirty minutes but finally turned to the college student and said, "Joe, you know, there are a lot of things I don't like about this!" Joe was astute enough to interpret this casual comment, and they both showed up at the back door about 1:00 A.M.

My son came by this fascination for the terrifying quite naturally. His mother is quite addicted to the best (or worst) Hollywood horror movies. My wife loves to view such movies, but unfortunately she cannot abide to watch them alone. She requests my companionship during her viewing pleasure, quite to my dismay. The result of such episodes is that my wife is left in a state of veritable horror, and I emerge brutally bruised by her clutching and grasping of me in her fear.

Thus we are fearful, yet fascinated by the Holy. We can approach it, and we want to, yet we must somehow keep a safe distance from it. We deal with it, but only after camouflaging some of its terror.

THE THREAT OF DISINTEGRATION

Otto's analysis has shown that the human experience with the Holy produces a variety of shocks. This traumatic character of the encounter can be summarized as involving a positive threat of disintegration. Man's self-image, individually and collectively, experiences a clear and present danger in the presence of the Holy. The sense of contrast immediately imposed is devastating to human security. Calvin notes this with particular reference to biblical accounts of such encounters:

Hence that dread and amazement with which the Scripture uniformly relates. Holy men were struck and overwhelmed whenever they beheld the presence of God. When we see those who previously stood firm and secure quaking with fear that the fear of death takes hold of them, they are in a manner, swallowed up and annihilated.—The inference to be drawn is this: that men are never duly touched and impressed with a conviction of their insignificance until they have contrasted themselves with the majesty of God.—Frequent examples of this consternation occur both in the Book of Judges and the Prophetical Writings so much so that it was a common expression of the people of God, "we shall die, for we have seen the Lord." Their folly, their feebleness and their pollution always derives its chief argument from descriptions of the Divine wisdom, virtue and purity. . . . Nor without God—for we see Abraham ready to acknowledge himself but dust and ashes the nearer he approaches the glory of the Lord; and Elijah unable to wait with unveiled face for his approach so dreadful is the sight. And what can man do—man who is but rottenness and a worm, when even the cherubim must veil their faces in very terror. To this undoubtedly the Prophet Isaiah refers when he says the moon shall be confounded and the sun ashamed when the Lord of Hosts shall reign. When he shall exhibit his refulgence and give a nearer view of it, the brightest objects will in comparison be covered with darkness.[11]

It is interesting to compare Otto's analysis of human reactions to the Holy with John Calvin's descriptions of the feeling-states of the biblical characters alluded to. Calvin notes feelings of dread, amazement, a loss of a sense of firmness and security, a sense of fear (quaking), being swallowed up, annihilation, consternation, a fear of death, a sense of folly, feebleness, and pollution, a sense of worthlessness (dust and ashes), a sense of dread, terror, confoundedness, and shame. These are not pleasant sensations for the normal person. The masochist might delight in them, but the average man would not particularly enjoy them. If finding God involves these experiences, who would deliberately seek Him? Who wants to experience the loss of security and a sense of annihilation?

Let us examine more closely some of the episodes Calvin mentions. First is the case of Habakkuk the prophet. Like Job, Habakkuk was perplexed over the problem of evil and suffering. He begins his oracle with a lament of anguish.

How long, O LORD, will I call for help, and Thou wilt not hear? I cry out to Thee, "Violence!" Yet Thou dost not save. Why dost Thou make me see iniquity, and cause me to look on wickedness? Yes, destruction and violence are before me; strife exists and contention arises. Therefore, the law is ignored and justice is never upheld. For the wicked surround the righteous; therefore, justice comes out perverted. (Habakkuk 1:2-4)

The lament is followed by withdrawal to a watchtower to await the answer of God. When God responds and gives answer to his inquiry, Habakkuk exclaims,

I heard and my inward parts trembled; at the sound my
lips quivered. Decay enters my bones, and in my place I
tremble. (Habakkuk 3:16)

In encounter with God, Habakkuk becomes a man of trembling belly and quivering lips. What does it mean to experience a sense of decay or rottenness entering into one's bones?

Perhaps even more exemplary of the human experience of the sense of disintegration is found in the classic encounter of Isaiah with the majesty of God. Isaiah relates it in the following terms:

In the year of King Uzziah's death, I saw the Lord sitting
on a throne, lofty and exalted, with the train of His robe
filling the temple. Seraphim stood above Him, each having
six wings; with two he covered his face, and with two he cov-
ered his feet, and with two he flew. And one called out to
another and said, "Holy, Holy, Holy, is the LORD of hosts, the
whole earth is full of His glory." And the foundations of the
thresholds trembled at the voice of him who called out, while
the temple was filling with smoke. Then I said, "Woe is me,
for I am ruined! Because I am a man of unclean lips, and
I live among a people of unclean lips; for my eyes have seen
the King, the LORD of hosts." (Isaiah 6:1-5)

Isaiah's response begins with an exclamation of woe. This "woefulness" reflects an experience of a sense of doom. In prophetic oracles, the oracle of woe involves the announcement of the awful, impending judgment of God. The pronouncement of woe is not positive but negative; it is not good news but bad news. As the Old Testament prophets use the "woe formula" to preface the divine indictment on Israel, so Jesus uses it to preface His scathing judgment on the Pharisees of His day. "Woe unto you, scribes, and Pharisees, hypocrites! How can you possibly escape the judgment of hell." The woe saying functions in contrast with the utterances of blessing as found in the Beatitudes. The blessing formula is benediction; the woe formula is malediction.

In the temple Isaiah's prophetic utterance is directed inwardly. He pronounces the woe of God not on the external enemies of Israel, not on the hypocrites around him, but in the presence of the majesty of God, he pronounces the malediction on himself—"Woe is me!" In this pronouncement Isaiah expresses the feeling of calamity. He has been exposed to the majesty of God, and the fear of death comes upon him. He says "woe" because he feels "ruined" or "undone." Vos says of this, "This is a sense, not of general fear, but of moral dissolution."[12]

Thus, in Isaiah's case, the feeling of being undone, or dissolved, or disintegrated accompanies his vision of the holiness of God. In contemporary nomenclature we use terms like "coming apart at the seams," "falling apart," "going to pieces," "being shattered," "coming unglued," "losing one's cool," to describe this type of experience. To come apart is to be disintegrated. The loss of a sense of being "integrated" or of "having it all together" produces insecurity and instability. To overcome these feeling-states, men seek to be "whole." The threat of disintegration or dissolution is a serious one to man. The holiness of God manifests that threat to the utmost.

The disintegrating factor in Isaiah's experience is not difficult to ascertain. His self-image is destroyed as he faces himself in the light of absolute holiness. The manifestation of God's holiness functions as the supreme iconoclast. In his encounter with God, Isaiah not only apprehends something about God but he also apprehends something about Isaiah. His vision of God brings with it a new vision of himself. In this experience Isaiah's ego is not simply bruised but is smashed. And thus he feels "undone."

The self-realization that accompanies the sense of disintegration is expressed in terms of a loss of a sense of purity. He says, "I am a man of unclean lips." This loss of cleanness or purity has an obvious moral referent. In the presence of the Holy, Isaiah feels dirty. The sense of filth, of dirt, of uncleanness is a common human feeling associated with moral guilt. When guilt feelings are resolved in the counter experience of forgiveness, men frequently use such images as being made clean or fresh or "white as snow." The feeling of being clean is a positive moral feeling; the feeling of being dirty or filthy is clearly a negative feeling. Isaiah's experience would not be the focus of delight of the hedonist. It is an experience of pain, not of pleasure.

It is interesting that Isaiah's encounter with holiness did not leave him with a "holier-than-thou" attitude. His conversion was not to hypocrisy, but from it. Yet at the same time he did not experience his awareness of moral corruption in isolation from its corporate ramifications. When Isaiah realized that his own lips were dirty, he recognized at the same time that this condition was not unique with him. He says, "I am a man of unclean lips, and I dwell in the midst of a people of unclean lips." Isaiah recognized in the context of traumatic shock that a contrast existed not simply between God and Isaiah, but between God and all mankind. Isaiah saw himself on the side of the unholy, the impure, the unclean.

To be sure, God did not leave Isaiah in his state of woe. He didn't leave him in dis-integration. The account goes on to relate that God dealt with Isaiah's dirty mouth. A red-hot coal was taken from the altar of the temple and placed on Isaiah's lips. The imagery of that episode is indeed awesome. This must have been a moment of considerable pain. Isaiah underwent purification and refinement by fire. In a word, his diseased lips were cauterized. Out of the pain, however, came healing, and Isaiah left the temple an integrated man.

The New Testament provides similar experiences involving the disciples of Jesus. We have the stories of several experiences of fear that may be helpful to our investigation. The first involves fear in the context of the threat of natural forces.

And leaving the multitude, they took Him along with them, just as He was, in the boat; and other boats were with Him.

And there arose a fierce gale of wind, and the waves were breaking over the boat so much that the boat was already filling up. And He Himself was in the stern, asleep on the cushion; and they awoke Him and said to Him, "Teacher, do You not care that we are perishing?" And being aroused, He rebuked the wind and said to the sea, "Hush, be still." And the wind died down and it became perfectly calm. And He said to them, "Why are you so timid? How is it that you have no faith?" And they became very much afraid and said to one another, "Who then is this, that even the wind and the sea obey Him?" (Mark 4:36-41)

This narrative relates an experience involving human fear before the threatening forces of nature. Here men are faced with the perils of a storm at sea, which includes the threat of annihilation. In the face of the threat of nature the men were described as being afraid. Yet when the threat of nature was removed, the fear was not. Rather than being eliminated or diminished, the fear of the men was accentuated. The awesome manifestation of the power of Jesus was more terrifying than the storm. In this case the power of the one whose power transcends the force of nature is more threatening than the power He transcends. The personal, when it is the personal Holy, threatens more than the impersonal.

Freud's thesis that men are less threatened by the personal than the impersonal cannot go unchallenged. It may be generally true that personal or personalized natural forces are less threatening to man than impersonal forces. (The idea rests on the notion that, being persons ourselves, we can more easily deal with personal forces because we have considerable experience and practice dealing with persons and also some degree of understanding of personal responses.) However, when the quality of holiness is added to the personal, it is no longer on a common plane with us. Perhaps it can be summarized this way: The nonholy personal may not threaten or be somewhat threatening. The nonholy impersonal threatens more. The Holy personal threatens most. Stated another way, the unholy personal is most desirable, the non-holy, impersonal is less desirable, and the Holy personal is least desirable. We may understand and be able to cope with the nonholy personal (men) or the nonholy impersonal (nature), but the Holy personal (the divine) is more foreign and alien to us than anything. We are, in effect, alienated by the alien. We are so unlike the Holy that it intimidates us. The instinctive human fear of strangers is even more pronounced in the encounter between the human and the divine.

Thus the moral qualitative difference that exists between man and God is greater than the difference that exists between man and nature. His alienation toward God is greater than his alienation toward nature simply because there is a greater degree of "alienness" in God than there is in nature. We share creaturehood with nature but not with God. The qualitative difference between Creator and creature is an unbridgeable chasm. The essential foreign element in God is to be found in His holiness. Psalm 50:21 makes the situation clear: God says to unrighteous man, "You thought that I was just like you; I will reprove you."

HUMAN REACTION TO THE HOLINESS OF CHRIST

The response of the disciples to Jesus in the episode of the calming of the sea is not atypical. A further illustration of the threatening character of Jesus may be seen in an incident involving Peter.

And He saw two boats lying at the edge of the lake; but the fishermen had gotten out of them, and were washing their nets. And He got into one of the boats, which was Simon's, and asked him to put out a little way from the land. And He sat down and began teaching the multitudes from the boat. And when He had finished speaking, He said to Simon, "Put out into the deep water and let down your nets for a catch." And Simon answered and said, "Master, we worked hard all night and caught nothing, but at Your bid-

*ding I will let down the nets." And when they had done
this, they enclosed a great quantity of fish; and their nets
began to break; and they signaled to their partners in the
other boat for them to come and help them. And they came,
and filled both of the boats, so that they began to sink. But
when Simon Peter saw that, he fell down at Jesus' feet, saying, "Depart from me, for I am a sinful man, O Lord!" For
amazement had seized him and all his companions because
of the catch of fish which they had taken. (Luke 5:2-9)*

Here Peter's reaction to the power of Jesus over nature is
somewhat startling. We can readily understand his astonish-
ment at the work Jesus performed, but what was it that
made him ask Jesus to leave? Suddenly Jesus was unwelcome
in the presence of Peter. Why? One would think that Peter's
reaction would be to implore Jesus to sign on as a member of
the crew. But Peter asked Him to leave. He said, "Depart
from me, for I am a sinful man!" Peter glimpsed more than
naked power in Jesus' mighty act. Peter recognized the holiness present in Christ and the intrusion of the "otherness" of
the Holy made Peter uncommonly uncomfortable. Like Isaiah
before him, Peter saw himself in contrast to Jesus, and he
didn't like what he saw.

Perhaps no human being in the history of the world has
received more praise and respect from men than Jesus of
Nazareth. Even many who deny His claims to deity speak
well of Him. John Gerstner has pointed out,

*The virgin reaction and all the subsequent reactions of the
world to Jesus Christ is, then, that He is the ideal, the perfect man, the moral paragon of the race. I do not wish to
gloss over the fact that not absolutely everyone has agreed
with this verdict. I know that George Bernard Shaw spoke of
a time in Christ's life when, as he said, Christ was not a
Christian. I know that some have thought that Socrates died
more nobly than Jesus: that others believe Him to have been
morally surpassed. But the overwhelming testimony of the*

world is to the perfection, the incomparable perfection, of Jesus of Nazareth. The few exceptions could easily be shown to rest on fundamental misconceptions of certain things which Jesus said or did; and furthermore, the vast majority of those who do take exception usually think that some imagined fault is a failure of Christ to be, as George Bernard Shaw said, a Christian! They seem to know of no higher standard by which to test Christ than the standard of Christ Himself. [13]

Other world religions have frequently spoken in glowing terms of Christ's moral excellence, and some have even sought to incorporate Him somehow into their own religious systems. Yet with all this applause, the fact remains that Jesus was killed by His contemporaries. He is praised in the distance of time, but was intolerable to His contemporaries.

THE THREAT OF MORAL EXCELLENCE

It is a common occurrence among social human beings that a person who manifests a superior excellence is resented by his contemporaries. The student who consistently breaks the curve of the academic grading system is frequently treated with quiet hostility by his classmates. Part of the now famous Peter Principle is that it is not only the super-incompetent person who is doomed to failure within the hierarchical structure of large corporations. The super-competent individual also faces the grim prospect of limited success by virtue of his very level of competence. The unusually competent person represents a threat not only to his peers but to his superiors as well, and is frequently treated as persona non grata.

These cases illustrate the fact that, in most hierarchies, super-competence is more objectionable that incompetence.
    Ordinary incompetence, as we have seen, is not cause for dismissal; it is simply a bar to promotion. Super-competence

often leads to dismissal, because it disrupts the hierarchy,
and thereby violates the first commandment of hierarchal
life: the hierarchy must be preserved.[14]

Competency at a moral level is perhaps the most unwelcome kind of competency. The clergyman frequently functions
as a symbol of moral competency. In spite of some recent
scandals involving noted Christian leaders, in the minds of
many people the clergyman is still a symbol of the sanctity of
the church and is viewed with a kind of "innocence by associ-
ation." The Dutch have a strange idiom to express this.
When a group of people are engaged in vigorous and animat-
ed conversation which suddenly and abruptly halts momentar-
ily, and an awkward silence prevails, someone will break the
silence by uttering *Loopt een dominee bij* ("A minister
walked by"). That is, because the appearance of a minister in
real situations can inhibit free, spontaneous discourse and
thus produce an awkward silence, any time an awkward silence occurs (even when no minister is near) the Dutchman
says, "A minister walked by." That his presence can evoke a
sense of inhibition and discomfort (no matter what he says or
does) is common knowledge to any clergyman.

If clergymen or other people are imagined to be in a special class of moral excellence and are thus especially inhibiting
and intimidating to their fellow men, how much more inhibiting and intimidating was Christ? At the calming of the sea
the final query of the disciples was, "What manner of man is
this, that even the winds and the sea obey Him?" What kind
of man was Jesus? His contemporaries could not find an ade-
quate class or category in which to pigeonhole Him. He
manifested Himself as the supreme *sui generis.* He was not
only different; He was unique.

The unique moral excellence of Jesus was a massive threat
to His contemporaries, particularly to those who were considered to be the moral elite of His day. It was the Pharisees
(those "set apart" to righteousness) who were most hostile to

Jesus. Though the popular masses hailed the Pharisees for their moral excellence, Jesus exposed them as hypocrites. He "broke their curve," providing a new standard under which the old standard of morality dissolved. Jesus disintegrated the firm security of His contemporaries. When the Holy appeared, the pseudo-holy were exposed.

The holy and the pure are indirectly destructive forces, forces of disintegration. Absolute holiness, purity, and innocence cannot be tolerated because they are dangerous and destructive. Perhaps one of the most poignant examples of this phenomenon may be seen in the character of Lennie in John Steinbeck's *Of Mice and Men.*

Lennie is portrayed as a man of enormous physical size with the mind and emotions of a child. His brute strength is exceeded in degree only by his simplistic innocence. Eking out an existence as a migrant worker, Lennie manifests a tender affection for little furry animals such as rabbits and mice. His concern for the well-being of these creatures is abnormal. He has an uncontrollable love for them that is expressed by holding them in his gargantuan hands and fondling and stroking them at length. However, Lennie's abnormal behavior frightens the animals, and in their panic they seek to squirm out of his grasp. In his innocence, Lennie grasps the creatures more tightly in an effort to show his love more deeply. However, Lennie is oblivious to his own strength; and in his effort to demonstrate his affection, he crushes the animals to death.

The peculiar quirk of Lennie's personality provides nothing more than annoyance to Lennie's companion and guardian, George. No great harm is done until Lennie falls in love, not with another rabbit or mouse, but with a woman. One of the worker's wives tries to seduce Lennie, luring him on with soft hair made up in sausage curls. She invites Lennie to stroke her hair but panics when Lennie's stroke becomes too hard. Suddenly she seeks to leave him, turning on him with cruel insults. Bewildered, Lennie tries to hold her to show his deep love for her. Steinbeck writes,

She struggled violently under his hands. Her feet battered on the hay and she writhed to be free; and from under Lennie's hand came a muffled screaming. Lennie began to cry with fright. "Oh! Please don't do none of that," he begged. "George gonna say I done a bad thing. He ain't gonna let me tend no rabbits." He moved his hand a little and her hoarse cry came out. Then Lennie grew angry. "Now don't," he said. "I don't want you to yell. You gonna get me in trouble jus' like George says you will. Now don't you do that." And she continued to struggle, and her eyes were wild with terror. He shook her then, and he was angry with her. "Don't you go tellin'," he said, and he shook her; and her body flopped like a fish. And then she was still, for Lennie had broken her neck.[15]

With this incident Lennie's idiosyncrasies were no longer tolerable. George whisked Lennie away with a posse in swift pursuit. Lennie had no real understanding of the enormity of his crime. He babbled repeatedly like a child, "I done a bad thing. . . ." Finally with the posse at their heels, George pointed beyond the river to an imaginary farm where there awaited for Lennie a multitude of rabbits, mice, puppies and other furry creatures. As Lennie stood transfixed by the conjured visin, contemplating endless hours of showing his unreserved affection, George calmly and deliberately blew his brains out with a revolver. When the posse arrived, one of the men reflected to George, "Never you mind. . . . A guy got to sometimes."

Lennie was a freak. His abnormal affection made him intolerable to society. His love was the kind that was both tender and brutal. He destroyed the objects of his affection because he loved them more than they wanted to be loved. The power of his love evoked fear in them and consequently they sought with all of their might to flee from them. Many have seen in Steinbeck's "Lennie" a dramatic Christlike figure. While the parallels cannot be extended too far, it is obvious from the story of Lennie—and much more so, of course, in the story of Christ—that abnormal love cannot be tolerated. It leaves man and beast in a state of traumatic discomfort.

COSMIC CLAUSTROPHOBIA

Another dimension of the holiness of God which provokes a negative human response is the dimension of God's glory. The concept of God's glory is inseparably related to holiness. In biblical categories, the glory of God is expressed in the Old Testament word *kabod* and the New Testament *doxa*. The corresponding Latin term is *dignitas* from which our English *dignity* derives.

In the Old Testament *kabod* is used in close connection with the word *qodesh* ("holy"). Though the two are closely related, they can be distinguished. Old Testament scholar Edmond Jacob says of God's *kabod*:

This glory is what God possesses in his own right, it is a kind of totality of qualities which make up his divine power; it has a close affinity with the holiness which is of the nature of deity and it is a visible extension for the purpose of manifesting holiness to men. Whether it be manifest in the sphere of creation, history or the cultus, it is always . . . uncovered holiness."[16]

The root meaning of kabod is "weighty," "heavy," or "important." The word is sometimes used to describe man as well as God. Just as we speak frequently of the dignity of man, so the Bible speaks of man's glory. The glory of man is located in his importance and prestige in the cosmos.

When the glory of man is related to the glory of God, there is a marked contrast. In the context of the glory of God, human glory is dwarfed by comparison. The weightiness of divine glory presses in upon man, threatening to crowd him out.

Throughout the Old Testament, the glory of God represents an awesome manifestation of God's being. The image of

the thunderstorm is frequently used to point to God's glory.
Glory is always somewhat veiled. Direct access to it is de-
nied. God's glory is glimpsed here in the pillar of cloud and
there in the flaming sword; but an unveiled, unobscured vision cannot be endured by human eyes.

Even Moses, in his privileged position of being the media-
tor of the Old Covenant, is not permitted to gaze directly at
the glory of God.

*Then Moses said, "I pray Thee, show me Thy glory!" And
He said, "I Myself will make all My goodness pass before
you, and will proclaim the name of the LORD before you;
and I will be gracious to whom I will be gracious, and will
show compassion on whom I will show compassion." But He
said, "You cannot see My face, for no man can see me and
live!" Then the LORD said, "Behold, there is a place by Me,
and you shall stand there on the rock; and it will come
about, while My glory is passing by, that I will put you in
the cleft of the rock and cover you with My hand until I
have passed by. Then I will take My hand away and you
shall see My back, but my face shall not be seen." (Exodus
33:18-23)*

Here Moses is allowed to see the back of God, but a direct
frontal view of His glory is prohibited.

Even this direct viewing of God's glory presents problems
for Moses as he returns to speak with the people of Israel.
When Moses descended from his encounter with God on
Mount Sinai, his face shone in a way that reflected the glory
of God. The sight of Moses terrified the people.

*So when Aaron and all the sons of Israel saw Moses, behold,
the skin of his face shone, and they were afraid to come
near him. . . . When Moses had finished speaking with
them, he put a veil over his face. But whenever Moses went
in before the LORD to speak with Him, he would take off the
veil until he came out; and whenever he came out and*

*spoke to the sons of Israel what he had been commanded, the
sons of Israel would see the face of Moses, that the skin of
Moses' face shone. So Moses would replace the veil over his
face until he went in to speak with Him. (Exodus 34:30,
33-35)*

In the New Testament the concept of the glory of God is
rendered by the Greek *doxa* (from which the English term
doxology derives). One of the astonishing factors in the New
Testament is the way in which the term is used in connection
with Jesus. John says concerning Jesus,

*And the Word became flesh, and dwelt among us, and we
beheld His glory, glory as of the only begotten from the Father, full of grace and truth. (John 1:14)*

Perhaps what John refers to in his prologue in terms of be-
holding the glory of Christ is the Transfiguration. The account of this episode in the life of Jesus is a very puzzling
one. What is clearly implied by the text, however, is that the
disciples were afforded an unparalleled glimpse of the glory of
Christ. Luke says,

*And some eight days after these sayings, it came about that
He took along Peter and John and James, and went up to
the mountain to pray. And while He was praying, the
appearance of His face became different, and His clothing
became white and gleaming. And behold, two men were
talking with Him; and they were Moses and Elijah, who,
appearing in glory, were speaking of His departure which
He was about to accomplish at Jerusalem. . . . And while
He was saying this, a cloud formed and began to oversha-
dow them; and they were afraid as they entered the cloud.
(Luke 9:28-34)*

The appearance of Christ in glory is an awesome thing.
The biblical writers speak of the "weight of His glory." This

weightiness is the subject of the churches' doxology and of the pagans' hostility. In the great Christological controversies of the fourth century, the church saw an inseparable relationship between doxology and the confession of the deity of Christ. Out of the struggle with the Arian heresy the Gloria Patri emerged as a "fight song" for those who saw the Son as part of the divine Trinity. The song contained the words "Glory be to the Father, and to the Son, and to the Holy Ghost." The threefold ascription of glory was a confessional formula for the Trinity.

Throughout the history of the church the glory of God has remained as a focal point of praise and adoration. To the non-Christian, however, it has been the focus of cosmic claustrophobia. The weightiness and heaviness of God have been felt as a crushing power that men would prefer to "make light of." The mocking of God is seen biblically as a failure to take seriously His dignity—His *kabod*—His glory. Thus the weightiness of God's glory is part of the trauma of holiness.

Holiness is intimidating, whether we discern it in a human being or encounter the Holy directly. The Bible does not try to conceal the fact that, in spite of God's love and mercy, He is an awesome, threatening Being, a Being that man would not instinctively search for. The psychologists continue to argue that men like to invent protective deities that will provide them with comfort and security. But they cannot argue that men would invent the intimidating Holy One of Israel. There are many reasons why men would witness to the existence and activity of the Holy One—one reason being that He actually exists—but mere need and imagination are not valid reasons.

NOTES

1. Mircea Eliade, *The Sacred and Profane,* trans. William R. Trask (New York: Harper & Row, 1957), 8.
2. Rudolf Otto, *The Idea of the Holy,* trans. John W. Harvey (New York: Oxford University Press, 1958).
3. Ibid., 7.
4. Otto sharply distinguishes between what he means by creature-feeling and

Friedrich Schleiermacher's notion of "feeling of dependence" and is critical of William James's analysis in *Varieties of Religious Experience*.

5. Otto, *Idea of the Holy,* 10.
6. Ibid., 14.
7. Geerhardus Vos, *Biblical Theology* (Grand Rapids: Eerdmans, 1948), 96. Cf. Edmond Jacob, *Theology of the Old Testament,* trans. Arthur W. Heathcote and Philip J. Allcock (New York: Harper & Brothers, 1958), 47.
8. Eliade, *Sacred and Profane,* 23.
9. Otto, *Idea of the Holy,* 23.
10. Ibid., 31.
11. John Calvin, *Institutes of the Christian Religion,* vol. 1, trans. Henry Beveridge (Grand Rapids: Eerdmans, 1964), 39.
12. Vos, *Biblical Theology,* 267.
13. John H. Gerstner, *Reasons for Faith* (New York: Harper & Brothers, 1960), 81.
14. Laurence J. Peter and Raymond Hull, *The Peter Principle* (New York: Bantam, 1969), 28.
15. John Steinbeck, *Of Mice and Men* (New York: Modern Library, 1937), 158.
16. Jacob, *Theology of the Old Testament,* 79-80.

CHAPTER 6
GOD AND THE FEAR OF NAKEDNESS

One of the most fascinating arguments against the existence of God ever developed has come from the pen of French author Jean-Paul Sartre. Sartre, who died in 1980, showed an uncanny ability to penetrate the inward throbbings of human feeling and reactions to life situations. Holding to a natural view of man and the world and denying the existence of God, Sartre reversed the order of classical idealism, rationalism, and essentialism with his famous slogan, "Existence precedes essence."

With the notion of the priority of existence over essence, Sartre took issue with all who sought to understand the particular in light of the universal, the individual in light of the group. He began his critique of theism at the point of the Christian concept of creation of man by a divine act. If God produced men in a similar fashion to the method employed by a human artisan, then, said Sartre, He created man according to some preconceived idea of "humanness," to which the created reality corresponded or conformed. Hence, in creation, man's "existence" would be threatened by the priority of "essence" as it flows from the consciousness of God.[1]

In analyzing human existence, Sartre rooted the uniqueness of man in his being a subject rather than an object. It is precisely at the point of man's subjectivity that Sartre offered a unique critique of the existence of God. He introduced the notion of the "look" or the "gaze" that threatens the existence of men by seeking to reduce them to the level of objects.

Perhaps no philosopher has provided a more convincing analysis of the dynamics of the experience of being "looked at" than Sartre. In *Being and Nothingness* Sartre devoted an entire section to the experience of "The Look." In this section he used as his basic model the scenario of a man who looks through a keyhole at someone and is caught in his act of voyeurism by another.

But all of a sudden I hear footsteps in the hall. Someone is looking at me! What does this mean? It means that I am suddenly affected in my being and that essential modifications appear in my structure—modifications which I can apprehend and fix conceptually by means of the reflective cogito.[2]

The experience of being beneath the gaze or the look of another includes elements of shame, fear, and, possibly, pride. Sartre devoted most of his attention to the experience that he called "shame-consciousness." This shame does not take place in a vacuum. Rather, shame is experienced in the presence of another. In this experience my subjectivity is reduced to objectivity as I become the object of the gaze or scrutiny of the other. I lose mastery of the situation and experience shame. Sartre says,

Similarly, shame is only the original feeling of having my being outside, engaged in another being and as such without any defense, illuminated by the absolute light which emanates from a pure subject. Shame is the consciousness of being irremediably what I always was: "in suspense"— that is, in the mode of the "not yet" or of the "already-no-longer." Pure shame is not a feeling of being this or that guilty object but in general of being an object; that is, of rec-

ognizing myself in this degraded, fixed, and dependent be-ing which I am for the Other. Shame is the feeling of an original fall, not because of the fact that I may have com-mitted this or that particular fault but simply that I have "fallen" into the world in the midst of things and that I need the mediation of the Other in order to be what I am.[3]

Thus, for Sartre, "shame-consciousness" is bound up with being in the presence of the Other. "Shame is a unitary ap-prehension with three dimensions: I am ashamed of myself before the Other."[4] Coming under the gaze of another is dan-gerous business, as my subjectivity is at stake, and my free-dom from shame is threatened.

Sartre dramatized the threatening character of coming un-der the gaze of the Other in his best-known play, *No Exit.* The play involves four characters confined to a room in which no mirrors are available, and the people are left to the experience of communicating with each other. The setting of the drawing room depicts Sartre's portrait of hell. What ap-pears as a pleasant setting for social intercourse finally be-comes an environment for mutual hatred. The oft-quoted punch line of the play is uttered by the character Garcin.

This bronze. (Strokes it thoughtfully.) *Yes, now's the moment: I'm looking at this thing on the mantelpiece, and I under-stand that I'm in hell. I tell you, everything's been thought out beforehand. They knew I'd stand at the fireplace strok-ing this thing of bronze, with all those eyes intent on me. Devouring me.* (He swings round abruptly.) *What? Only two of you? I thought there were more; many more.* (Laughs.) *So this is hell. I'd never have believed it. You remember all we were told about the torture-chambers, the fire and brimstone, the "burning marl." Old wives' tales! There's no need for red-hot pokers. Hell is—other people![5]*

"Hell is other people!"—this line is the climactic moment of the play. Yet frequently a more subtle point of the drama is lost by the revelation of Garcin. It is found in the final stage directive of the text.

(They slump onto their respective sofas. A long silence. Their laughter dies away and they gaze at each other.)[6]

If Sartre found the experience of being subjected to the gaze of other people repugnant, how much more hellish did he regard the gaze of God? For Sartre, God implied not so much an "Unmoved Mover" as an "Unviewed Viewer." That is, God is the ultimate Other who has the capacity of omniscience, whereby He keeps everyone beneath His gaze, while at the same time no one may gaze at Him. God is the cosmic voyeur who has no fear of being discovered at His celestial keyhole by another. Beneath God's gaze we are all reduced to absolute objects and have our humanity destroyed. Thus, for Sartre, if man exists as a subject, God cannot exist.

EXISTENTIAL SELF-AWARENESS
Analysis of self-awareness is not unique with Sartre. It has been the subject of considerable interest in modern culture, as indicated by the popular receptivity of Julius Fast's book *Body Language*. In this volume the author provides an analysis of ways in which human beings indulge in nonverbal communication. Numerous variations of the position of the eyelid and eyebrow, the posture of standing at ease, and the dynamics of other bodily gestures are all noted as part of man's tools of communication. Of special interest, however, is the nature and the function of the human stare.

Fast points out the difference between the acceptable and the unacceptable stare. One can stare for long periods at monkeys in the zoo, or at paintings in a museum, with impunity. But to stare at a man in public with the same intensity or duration is to risk a bloody nose. Our cultural mores consider prolonged staring at human beings as involving an exercise in discourtesy. Though eye contact is a necessary component of social conversation, there is a thin line between the friendly duration and intensity of such eye-contact and the threatening "stare." If a glance is held too long, it can provoke embarrassment or even hostility.

Stated simply, the stare is appropriate for objects, but not for personal subjects. To be the victim of a stare is to be threatened by depersonalization. To become an object under the gaze of another provokes discomfort. It is like being an insect under a scientist's lens. We speak of "feeling" someone's eyes upon us, of people "looking through us." Women complain of the male stare as making them feel as though they are being undressed. In acknowledging strangers, we must avoid staring at them, and yet we must also avoid ignoring them. To treat them as people rather than objects, we use a deliberate and polite inattention. We look at them long enough to make it quite clear that we see them, and then we look away. We are saying in body language, "I know you are there," and a moment later we add, "but I would not dream of intruding on your privacy."[7]

As one frequently involved in public speaking, I am aware of the threatening character of the stare. In a public speaking situation it is important for the speaker to maintain eye contact with his audience. Yet in that eye contact he must avoid staring for long at a particular person. If the Sunday morning preacher delivered his sermon by staring at a single member of the congregation throughout his sermon, he would be apt to lose a parishioner.

On the other hand, it is permissible for the members of the audience to keep their eyes fixed upon the speaker. This state of affairs can eaily provoke "existential self-awareness," especially if the speaker is given to the extemporaneous form of address. In my own experience I have found that as I am speaking, my mind is concentrating on what I am about to say next. However, if in the course of the address I notice someone in the audience peering at me intently, I can easily lose my train of thought via self-awareness. If I stop to consider that the people are analyzing not only my message but me, paying attention not only to my words but also to my mannerisms, clothing, hairstyle, I could not only lose my train of thought but could go raving mad. Every speaker must struggle, either consciously or unconsciously, to block from his mind the threatening character of being subjected to the scrutiny of the collective gaze of his audience.

When I feel people staring at me, I feel judgment. This is what makes public speaking so threatening. I must speak through the judgment to be effective. I must ignore it, rise above it. To fix it in my mind is to succumb to the terror of it.

The above illustrations suffice to indicate the complex dimensions of the phenomenon of the stare. The stare can make us uncomfortable. We can sense via the stare a loss of humanness. We can sense an invasion of our privacy. In a word, we can feel exposed, naked. Clothes, shower curtains, doors, and window shades testify to the human need to protect one's nakedness from the gaze of another person.

THE NAKEDNESS MOTIF OF WESTERN CULTURE

Nudity and semi-nudity are concerns of some fascination in the Western world. The rise in popularity of pornographic videos, skimpy bathing suits for both sexes, nude centerfolds, and nude beaches herald an almost adolescent preoccupation with nakedness. Yet shower curtains and window shades remain household staples. On the one hand we see a desire to view nudity or be naked, and on the other a desire to remain covered. Why the mystique over nudity?

The aspect of nakedness has figured widely in modern man's attempt at self-understanding. In psychological environs, the nude therapy session emerged years ago as a frequent motif of sensitivity training techniques. People are encouraged to experience a high level of "vulnerability" by exposing themselves physically to others in the group in a context of trust. "Being open" and "sharing" or "revealing" one's innermost feelings has been connected with nudity. To shed clothes (the physical covering) is to expose not only the body but to remove the defense or the "covering" of the human psyche. The small group movement in religious circles has also stressed such "vulnerability" or "openness" as being of therapeutic value to the soul. The hope of an experience of forgiveness or acceptance followed by small group confession has been widespread.

Some people who have experienced such vulnerability sessions either in a secular or church situation have testified enthusiastically to feelings of liberation—of being released from the curse of living in a state of concealment. Others have testified to experiencing great trauma from such self-exposure.

There remains a kind of paradoxical attitude among many people to the matter of nakedness. A kind of collective ambivalence seems to be manifest in our culture about nudity. On the one hand, there is an enormous desire to view the naked body and at the same time to conceal it. There is the exhilarating feeling of liberation that often accompanies the act of undressing, yet at the same time a sense of shame or embarrassment if caught unexpectedly in a nude state.

This paradoxical character of nakedness is reflected in Søren Kierkegaard's notion of man as the *Homo Absconditus.* For centuries theologians have operated with the concept of the *Deus Absconditus,* God who remains hidden and obscured from human knowledge, God who remains "unrevealed." (Isaiah 45:15 states, "Truly, Thou art a God who hides Himself, O God of Israel, Savior!") But Kierkegaard called attention to the need of an *Absconditus* dimension of man. On the one hand, Kierkegaard is sharply critical of the person who lives merely on the "aesthetic" or "spectator" plane of life, operating within the context of the concealment of a masquerade. For that person Kierkegaard demands a radical "unmasking" to expose the chimera. He says in *Either/Or,*

Life is a masquerade, you explain, and for you this is inexhaustible material for amusement; and so far, no one has succeeded in knowing you; for every revelation you make is always an illusion, it is only in this way you are able to breathe and prevent people from pressing importunately upon you and obstructing your respiration. Your occupation consists in preserving your hiding-place, and that you succeed in doing, for your mask is the most enigmatical of all. In fact you are nothing; you are merely relation. To a fond shepherdess you hold out a languishing hand, and instantly you are masked in all possible bucolic sentimentality. A reverend spiritual father you deceive with a brotherly kiss, etc. You yourself are nothing, an enigmatic figure on whose brow is inscribed Either/or.[8]

In this scathing critique of the dishonest spectator, Kierkegaard hurls a challenge:

Do you know that there comes a midnight hour when everyone has to throw off his mask? Do you believe that life will always let itself be mocked? Do you think you can slip away a little before midnight in order to avoid this? Or are you not terrified by it? I have seen men in real life who so long deceived others that at last their true nature could not reveal itself. I have seen men who played hide and seek so long that at last madness through them obtruded disgustingly upon others their secret thoughts which hitherto they had proudly concealed. . . . In every man there is something which to a certain degree prevents him from becoming perfectly transparent to himself; and this may be the case in so high a degree, he may be so inexplicably woven into relationships of life which extend far beyond himself that he almost cannot reveal himself. But he who cannot reveal himself cannot love, and he who cannot love is the most unhappy man of all.[9]

Thus Kierkegaard sees self-concealment as being inevitably self-destructive. The ability to expose or reveal oneself is critical to the ability to love.

It sounds as if Kierkegaard is asking us to "let it all hang out," to jump into a state of absolute vulnerability in a spirit of reckless abandon. But such is not the case. Kierkegaard, the "Gadfly," did not go about Denmark naked. Though he called for living in a passionate state of high-level risk, he preserved an island of hiddenness for himself and for all men. Man can never escape a certain measure of "existential solitude," nor should he. Solitude affords a place of hiddenness that is necessary for the human subject.

On the other hand, he often feels a need of solitude, which for him is a vital necessity—sometimes like breathing, at other times like sleeping. The fact that he feels this vital necessity more than other men is also a sign that he has a deeper nature. Generally the need of solitude is a sign that there is spirit in a man after all, and it is a measure for what spirit there is. The purely twaddling inhuman and too-human men are to such a degree without feeling for the need of solitude that, like a certain species of social birds (the so-called lovebirds), they promptly die if for an instant they have to be alone. As this little child must be put to sleep by a lullaby, so these men need the tranquilizing hum of society before they are able to eat, drink, sleep, pray, fall in love, etc. But in ancient times as well as in the Middle Ages people were aware of the need of solitude and had respect for what it signifies. In the constant sociability of our age, people shudder at solitude to such a degree that they know no other use to put it to but (oh, admirable epigram!) as a punishment for criminals. But after all it is a fact that in our age it is a crime to have spirit, so it is natural that such people, the lovers of solitude, are included in the same class with criminals.[10]

Kierkegaard sees a paradoxical dimension to human self-revelation. Analogous to the relationship in God between the notion of the *Deus Revelatus* and the *Deus Absconditus* is the act of human revelation that comes by indirect communication. Zuidema summarizes Kierkegaard by saying,

No single mode of expression is able to reveal or disclose the inner and individual character of the existence or being of the human self. All expression, all communication is in its very nature a withdrawal, a mystery, a hiddenness. Expression and communication distort that which one would express. This cannot be otherwise. For communication, even verbal communication, is an externalization, an objectivization and generalization. The individual becoming of internal and free existence does not disclose itself to objective discursive thought. Nor does it reveal or disclose its own intimacy through the self-revelation of the spoken word. It does not permit its self-disclosure through this spoken word. Revelation is concealment. The individual is inexpressible and imperceptible. Man lives incognito throughout his life.[11]

THE BIBLICAL MOTIF OF NAKEDNESS

The theme of nakedness plays a remarkable role in biblical literature. The importance of the nakedness motif is often overlooked. The state of nakedness is closely linked with the Hebrew concept of "knowing" in a complex variety of ways. We will explore the motif of nakedness in an attempt to relate its significance to Sartre's notion of the "glance" and Kierkegaard's notion of homo absconditus.

The Greek word *gumnos* (from which we get our word *gymnasium*) is used biblically in both a literal and figurative sense. In its literal sense it is capable of being translated as "naked," "unclothed," "badly clothed," or "stripped by force." In its figurative usage the term is capable of a wider variety of nuances. Such ideas as "unconcealed," "disclosed," or "manifest" are conveyed by the figurative sense of nakedness. The state of the soul apart from the body is described by the Greeks as a "naked state." Roman Emperor Hadrian at his death addressed his naked soul. Nakedness is mentioned in antiquity as part of the torment of the damned. In the Samaritan liturgy for the eve of the Day of Atonement the *goyim* (Gentiles) will be raised naked, whereas the righteous will rise again with clothes. Finally, there is the sense in which nakedness describes the state of the soul or inner man that is without preparation for the day of judgment.[12]

NOAH'S NAKEDNESS

One of the most fascinating and puzzling narratives of the Pentateuch is the account of Ham's violation of his father, Noah, by means of looking at his nakedness.

Then Noah began farming and planted a vineyard. And he drank of the wine and became drunk, and uncovered himself inside his tent. And Ham, the father of Canaan, saw the nakedness of his father, and told his two brothers outside. But Shem and Japheth took a garment and laid it upon both their shoulders and walked backward and covered the nakedness of their father; and their faces were turned away, so that they did not see their father's nakedness. When Noah awoke from his wine, he knew what his youngest son had done to him. So he said, "Cursed be Canaan; a servant of servants he shall be to his brothers." He also said, "Blessed be the LORD, the God of Shem; and let Canaan be his servant. May God enlarge Japheth, and let him dwell in the tents of Shem; and let Canaan be his servant." (Genesis 9:20-27)

In this strange account the descendants of Ham receive the curse of their patriarchal ancestor Noah because Ham looked on his father's nakedness. Conversely, Shem and Japheth receive blessing because they refused to gaze upon their nude father and because they provided a covering for him. Notice in the passage that the sin of Ham is not that he looked upon his father's drunkenness, nor that he made sport or ridicule of his father's condition. The sin is in the looking at the nakedness of his father.

To receive the patriarchal curse was indeed a serious matter for the Jew of antiquity. By contemporary standards,

Noah's judgment seems outrageous. To curse your son because he looks at your naked body seems like a measure of cruel and unjust punishment. Justice appears mutilated by a punishment that is more severe than the crime. How can we make sense out of this enigmatic narrative that violates our modern sense of crime and punishment? Perhaps some insight can be gained by a broader view of biblical attitudes toward nakedness.

THE OLD TESTAMENT LAW

The Levitical Law gives detailed prohibitions and prescriptions for punishment concerning nakedness. A sampling of the law provides the following applications of the general prohibition of adultery.

If there is a man who lies with his father's wife, he has uncovered his father's nakedness; both of them shall surely be put to death, their bloodguiltiness is upon them. (Leviticus 20:11)

In this passage incest involves an uncovering of the father's nakedness. That is, the nakedness of the husband is identified by law as being equated with the nakedness of the wife. To uncover a man's wife is seen as a stripping of the man himself. The same attitude of uncovering is indicated with respect to uncle, brother, and other blood relatives (Leviticus 20:20-21).

If there is a man who takes his sister, his father's daughter or his mother's daughter, so that he sees her nakedness and she sees his nakedness, it is a disgrace; and they shall be cut off in the sight of the sons of the people. He has uncovered his sister's nakedness; he bears his guilt. . . . You shall also not uncover the nakedness of your mother's sister or of your father's sister, for such a one has made naked his blood relative; they shall bear their guilt. (Leviticus 20:17, 19)

From these samplings from the Old Testament Law it is obvious that the Hebrews took the matter of nakedness very seriously.

Beyond the Law, concern is often expressed for the threatening and dreadful character of nakedness. In the midst of unspeakable misery, Job rents his garments and shaves his head crying: "Naked I came from my mother's womb, and naked I shall return there" (Job 1:21). Amos pronounces God's judgment on Israel in this way:

Flight will perish from the swift, and the stalwart will not strengthen his power, nor the mighty man save his life. He who grasps the bow will not stand his ground; the swift of foot will not escape, nor will he who rides the horse save his life. Even the bravest among the warriors will flee naked in that day," declares the LORD. (Amos 2:14-16)

Nakedness is seen as a thing of doom, used by God as a means of punishment for the wicked. To be "sent naked away" is to be stripped to the point of humiliation and emptiness.

NAKEDNESS IN THE NEW TESTAMENT

The concern for the threatening character of nakedness is not limited to the Old Testament. It appears frequently in the New Testament. Christ promised blessings to those who fed Him when He was hungry, provided drink and hospitality when He was thirsty and a stranger, visited Him in prison, and clothed Him when He was naked. When queried about this by His disciples, Jesus declared, "Truly I say to you, to the extent that you did it to one of these brothers of mine, even the least of them, you did it to me" (Matthew 25:40). Jesus makes the clothing of the naked a priority in the establishing of the Kingdom of God.

The question of Jesus' clothing at the time of His crucifixion is unclear. His garments were divided among His executioners but the temporal sequence is obscure. The implication is, however, that part of the ignominy of Christ's humiliation is that He was crucified naked, being made a public spectacle. The parallel with the lament of the psalmist is obvious.

For dogs have surrounded me; a band of evildoers has encompassed me; they pierced my hands and my feet. I can count all my bones. They look, they stare at me; they divide my garments among them, and for my clothing they cast lots. (Psalm 22:16-18)

The writer of Revelation records the warning of Christ to the church of Laodicea.

Because you say, "I am rich, and have become wealthy, and have need of nothing," and you do not know that you are wretched and miserable and poor and blind and naked, I advise you to buy from Me gold refined by fire, that you may become rich, and white garments, that you may clothe yourself, and that the shame of your nakedness may not be revealed, and eyesalve to anoint your eyes, that you may see. (Revelation 3:17-18)

Again in chapter 16 Christ says, "Blessed is the one who stays awake and keeps his garments, lest he walk about naked and men see his shame" (Revelation 16:15).

The above-mentioned passages indicate clearly that nakedness is not a desirable state. Shame, humiliation, ignominy, and doom are associated with the naked state. But the question remains, why all the fuss about nakedness? Why is there such a correlation between nudity and humiliation? Why is it that to be unclothed is to be reduced to ignominy? The answer to these questions must be found in the context of the biblical account of the fall of man.

NAKEDNESS AND THE FALL

In the Genesis narrative of the creation of man and woman, we have a very succinct summation given—perhaps a bit too succinct, leaving the reader with a mild sense of the abrupt:

And the LORD *God fashioned into a woman the rib which He had taken from the man, and brought her to the man. And the man said, "This is now bone of my bones, and flesh of my flesh; she shall be called Woman, because she was taken out of Man." For this cause a man shall leave his father and his mother, and shall cleave to his wife, and they shall become one flesh. (Genesis 2:22-24)*

At this point the creation narrative seems to reach a conclusion with the sanctification of the institution of marriage culminating in the union of man and woman. Yet the narrative does not cease at this point but seems to tack on a postscript that sounds a bit foreign to the context. Almost as an afterthought we read the statement, "And the man and his wife were both naked and were not ashamed" (Genesis 2:25).

"Naked and not ashamed"? It sounds like an afterthought, but it is obviously more than that. This description of the first couple in the state of innocence is a crucial transition to the narrative that follows: the narrative of the Fall. The author of Genesis provides us with a gripping study in contrast that focuses on the words "naked and not ashamed."

The account of the fall of man rehearses the episode of the temptation proffered by the serpent. When Adam and Eve succumb to the temptation and experience sin, their first reaction is a reaction to their own nakedness.

Then the eyes of both of them were opened, and they knew that they were naked; and they sewed fig leaves together and made themselves loin coverings. And they heard the sound of the LORD *God walking in the garden in the cool of the day, and the man and his wife hid themselves from the presence of the* LORD *God among the trees of the garden. (Genesis 3:7-8)*

Here the consciousness of Adam and Eve was not immediately directed toward thoughts of the serpent or the tree or even God. Their eyes were opened (as the serpent said they would be), but what they saw was their own nakedness. But they had not been previously blind. It wasn't that now they experienced the power of visual perception for the first time. Adam could see the nakedness of Eve very plainly before the Fall. Nor was he blinded to the observation of his own body. The "opening of their eyes" is of course a figurative description of an awareness of shame—what Sartre described as "shame-consciousness." Where previously they delighted in the sound of God as He walked in the cool of the day, now they were terrified by that sound. Where they previously stood secure and totally unembarrassed beneath the gaze of God, now they desperately sought refuge from His sight. Man's nakedness being once a sign of the glory of innocence becomes his greatest disgrace. Martin Luther remarks,

Similarly, man does not realize that the glory of nakedness was lost through sin. The fact that Adam and Eve walked about naked was their greatest adornment before God and all the creatures. Now, after sin, we not only shun the glance of men when we are naked, but we are even bashful in our own presence.[13]

The relationship between physical nakedness and spiritual exposure is clear in this passage. In hiding their nakedness from the vision of God, Adam and Eve were hiding themselves.

The rest of the narrative tells of God searching for His creatures, calling out to Adam, "Where are you?" Adam responds, "I heard the sound of Thee in the garden, and I was afraid because I was naked; so I hid myself." Under the interrogation of his Maker, Adam uses a desperately contrived cover-up ploy. He claims that he is hiding because he is afraid and that the reason for his fear is his nakedness. It was a perfectly "natural" explanation for the original act of *Homo Absconditus,* an explanation that sufficed only until God raised the next question, "Who told you that you were naked?" The ploy failed and Adam's sin was exposed to the gaze of God. For Adam and his progeny the trauma was unforgettable. Even Sartre remarks,

Modesty and, in particular, the fear of being surprised in a state of nakedness are only a symbolic specification of original shame; the body symbolizes here our defenseless state as objects. To put on clothes is to hide one's object-state; it is to claim the right of seeing without being seen; that is, to be pure subject. This is why the biblical symbol of the fall after the original sin is the fact that Adam and Eve "know that they are naked." The reaction to shame will consist exactly in apprehending as an object the one who apprehended my own object-state.[14]

With the experience of sin comes the awareness of shame-in-nakedness. Throughout biblical history the motif is carried on. Yet some startling things took place in Eden that are frequently overlooked. With the sin comes judgment, punishment, and expulsion from Eden. Man leaves the Garden under the curse of God. But he does not leave naked!

In light of the indictment of God for the act of transgression, we might expect that God would rudely drag Adam from his hiding place, tear away the fig leaf in an act of divine fury, and condemn the man to exposure and shame. We might justly expect God to reduce His creature to the unprotected state of pure objectivity, being constantly exposed to His wrathful gaze and the gaze of all creation. But He does not. The judgment is real; indeed, it is devastating—but it is not ultimate. We read in Genesis 3:21: "And the LORD God made garments of skin for Adam and his wife, and clothed them." In a word, God provided a hiding place for His embarrassed creature. God beheld Adam's nakedness and covered it. Beneath the gaze of God, Adam found loving concern, not annihilation. Adam experienced not only the stare of judgment but the benevolent gaze of love.

BEING KNOWN OF GOD

The threat of exposure, of being caught naked, is related to the ominous threat of being known as we are. Again, ambivalence is characteristic of the human attitude toward being known. We go to extraordinary pains to hide those things about ourselves of which we are ashamed, yet at the same time we yearn for a place of refuge where we can be fully known without fear, where we can be naked and unashamed. The thought of being known is both terrifying and desirable. The thought that "hell is other people" is not the isolated insight of a tormented playwright but the collective fear of Adam's seed.

The ambivalence toward being known is seen in the standard procedure of dating. The male and the female progress from the encounter of the first date to the moment of truth in the honeymoon suite. The first date involves the all-important first impression. The magic of mascara, mousse, deodorant, mouthwash, etc., is plied in a massive effort to conceal ugliness and emphasize (or imitate) beauty. The conversation is cautious, guarded from being too revealing. Making a good impression is the order of the day.

But if the first date is successful and the relationship progresses to a more serious level, a crisis state is soon reached. The crisis comes when the person realizes that the other is responding warmly and the question begins to plague the mind, *Is she responding to me or to the image I've carefully projected?* What follows is the trial. Little bits of hidden areas are revealed and confessions of sins committed "long ago and far away" are made. If the trial of "remote confession" is successful, then the lover moves closer to the rim of authentic self-exposure. What is sought is the experience of loving and being loved in truth rather than concealment. Some, however, as Kierkegaard observed, never pass the trial, as their fear of exposure is so great that it outweighs their desire to be known and loved. Some even marry, but only as a way of gaining a ticket to a perpetual game of hide and seek.

So it is with being known of God. Who isn't threatened, indeed intimidated, by the notion of an all-knowing deity? To consider the thought that my life knows no secrets from the penetrating eye of God may be most discouraging. Yet I want to be known; I need to be known: ambivalence.

This ambivalence is clearly shown in the Bible. Let David be the model. After his sin with Bathsheba, sin that included the indirect murder of her husband, David had so deceived himself about the extent of his guilt that he didn't even recognize himself in Nathan's parable until Nathan boldly declared, "Thou art the man!" David's deception had reached the level of self-deception. When the revelation came and David was exposed, it was painful for him. He cried out in contrition, "For I know my transgressions, and my sin is ever before me. Against Thee, and Thee only, I have sinned, and done what is evil in Thy sight" (Psalm 51). Here David acknowledges the reality of that guilt and notes two very important factors. First, he notes that the sin is ever before him. It hounds him and pursues him. He sees it wherever he goes. He cannot rid himself of the memory. Like Lady Macbeth, the spot is indelible. Second, he notes that he has done evil in the sight of God. David not only sees his sin but he realizes it hasn't escaped the notice of God. His shame before the nation was great, but not worthy of comparison with his shame before God.

David knows that God sees his sin, and this is unbearable. He cries, "Let the bones which Thou hast broken rejoice. Hide Thy face from my sins, and blot out all my iniquities." So threatening is the gaze of God that David begs God to cover his face, to look away, to let him hide. He asks God to "blot out," to erase his iniquity. He doesn't want to look at it anymore and he doesn't want God to look at it anymore. David comes with a broken and contrite heart, naked before God. The repentance is real. But in the agony of exposure David finds forgiveness. Out of that forgiveness comes another psalm. Now he sings,

O LORD, Thou hast searched me and known me. Thou dost know when I sit down and when I rise up; Thou dost understand my thought from afar. Thou dost scrutinize my path and my lying down, and art intimately acquainted with all my ways. Even before there is a word on my

tongue, behold, O Lord, Thou dost know it all. (Psalm 139:1-4)

In this psalm David acknowledges that there is no refuge from God. Wherever he flees, God penetrates. David is known, and known altogether. Yet the mood of the psalm is not one of lamentation nor even of resignation. No bitterness or frustration can be found in its lines. The psalm is an expression of praise and delight. David realizes consolation, not dread, from his awareness of being known. In forgiveness David experiences the benevolent gaze of God and learns what it means to be naked and unashamed. So positive is the experience that once threatened him that David exclaims,

Search me, O God, and know my heart; try me and know my anxious thoughts; and see if there be any hurtful way in me, and lead me in the everlasting way. (Psalm 139:23-24)

David grasped a lesson that is excruciatingly difficult for the sons of Adam: Being known of God is not the loss of humanity, but the glory of it. He sought relief from the glance of God but could not find it. When he acquiesced to that glance in the pain of repentance, he knew peace.

Like David, those estranged from God behave in a way that often resembles elements of the paranoia syndrome, "The wicked flee when no man pursues"; and as Luther stated, "The pagan trembles at the rustling of a leaf." Like the paranoid who imagines that someone is "out to get him," man lives in terror at the thought of being exposed before God. He imagines that his enemy has but one intent, to destroy him. However, as the paranoid man produces distortions of the enemy, so the guilty man projects upon God the worst of all possible intentions. But the true design of the gaze of God is to bring repentance and by repentance, life. (Francis Thompson's famous poem "The Hound of Heaven" pictures man fleeing breathlessly from the God he fears: "I fled him down the nights and down the days . . . ," but the poem ends with the realization that the Pursuer was really divine love, not an enemy.) But here the analogy of the paranoid breaks down. Where the paranoid's enemies are imagined, the divine enemy of the guilty man is real. The threat of judgment is not a charade but an ominous reality when there is no repentance.

To be known of God may mean to be exposed to His wrath. Yet without it there is no redemption. The experience of biblical characters is ironic. When they sin, they all fear the gaze of God. When they repent, they all desire to be known of God. In fact, the essence of redemption is understood in terms of being known of God. Christ warned His disciples,

Not everyone who says to Me, "Lord, Lord," will enter the kingdom of heaven; but he who does the will of My Father who is in heaven. Many will say to Me on that day, "Lord, Lord, did we not prophesy in Your name, and in Your name cast out demons, and in Your name perform many miracles?" And then I will declare to them, "I never knew you; depart from Me, you who practice lawlessness." (Matthew 7:21-23)

The threat of Christ to the hypocrite who uses His name to shield himself from exposure of his moral anarchy is that He will declare him an unknown entity. "I never knew you" is the threat of judgment. In the framework of Christ's understanding, the worst thing that could happen to a man is to be a stranger to Him, not to be known by Him. Like the namedropper who walks up to a celebrity in order to impress his friends only to have the celebrity make it clear that he knows nothing of the man, the hypocrite faces the humiliation of exposure.

Thus the issue of redemption does not center on the question of whether or not a man "knows" God, but whether or not God "knows" him. To be known of God involves coming out from behind the bushes to experience His benevolent gaze. Thus, for the Jew of the Old Testament and the Christian of the New Testament, redemption is tied up with being known of God. The essence of happiness is to be in the presence of the One whose gaze may be terrifying.

One of the most concrete methods of expressing this notion of happiness is contained in the classic Hebrew benediction.

May the LORD bless you and keep you; the LORD make His face shine on you, and be gracious to you; the LORD lift up His countenance on you, and give you peace. (Numbers 6:24-26)

In this benediction we find a wish expressed in the Hebrew literary form of parallelism. Via parallelism the same basic thought is expressed three times in three different ways. The structure is broken down as follows:

bless—keep
make His face shine—gracious
lift up His countenance—peace

The two elements of "blessing" and "keeping" are repeated in synonymous terms. The blessing is identified with the experience of coming under the gaze of God. To have God make His face shine on you and to lift up His countenance upon you is to know blessedness. For the Jew, the highest blessing is to have God look at you, not to overlook you.

A recurring motif of biblical literature is that motif which draws a parallel between the relationship of God and man and the human situation of marriage. Repeatedly we find the relationship between Israel and Yahweh, Christ and His church, expressed in terms of marriage. Israel is Yahweh's bride as is the New Testament church the Bride of Christ. Covenant violations and acts of disobedience are described in terms of *adultery, whoredom, harlotry.* At the heart of the analogy is the concept of "knowing."

When the Old Testament describes the act of sexual intercourse by the verb "to know," it is not being given to euphemism. Abraham knew his wife and she conceived. Isaac knew his wife. Likewise, Mary explains in the New Testament, "How can this be since I know no man?" Here the word *know* is not being used to express intellectual knowledge or acquaintance of someone. Rather, it expresses the zenith of human knowledge, the knowledge of intimacy.

The marriage estate is analogous to the divine-human relationship in many respects. Both involve covenant structures in which the mutual parties are bound to each other by commitment sealed with oaths. Both involve a possibility of knowing-in-intimacy. Both involve a "place" where man can be naked and unashamed. In the context of marriage, I enter into the most intimate of all human relationships. It is a relationship that involves a certain amount of risk. If the marriage is to work, it must involve not only the possibility of nakedness, but the necessity of it. Within marriage I not only may be naked, I must be. If I take the risk and expose myself and discover that my wife has seen my nakedness in all of its ramifications, and still loves me, then I experience at the human level something of what it means to be known of God.

THE COVERING OF THE NAKED

Within the biblical framework there exists not only a concern for nakedness per se, but a concern for the covering of that nakedness as well. We have seen the blessing given to the sons of Noah who covered their father's nakedness. We have seen the startling act of mercy on the part of God when He makes clothes for Adam and Eve. We have noted the mandate of Christ to His disciples to see to it that the naked be clothed. However, the total picture of "covering" transcends these matters of concrete clothing. In biblical categories of redemption the notion of "covering" takes on far-reaching theological significance.

As the threat of nakedness, of being uncovered, is an ominous warning of judgment, so the promise of salvation is often made in terms of "covering" that exposure. On the one hand we hear the warning of Christ.

Therefore do not fear them, for there is nothing covered that will not be revealed, and hidden that will not be known. (Matthew 10:26)

This general warning takes on fearful proportions in Jesus' lament over the women of Jerusalem.

Daughters of Jerusalem, stop weeping for Me, but weep for yourselves and for your children. For behold, the days are coming when they will say, "Blessed are the barren, and the wombs that never bore, and the breasts that never nursed." Then they will begin to say to the mountains, "Fall on us," and to the hills, "Cover us." (Luke 23:28-30)

These dreadful warnings of the future state of the unrepentant who will beg for any kind of covering, even that supplied by the shattering of the mountains, is balanced by a promise of a covering for the redeemed.

The Chronicler prays for the "clothing of salvation" (2 Chronicles 6:41). The prayer of the historian becomes the song of the prophet.

I will rejoice greatly in the Lord, My soul will exult in my God; for He has clothed me with garments of salvation, He has wrapped me with a robe of righteousness, as a bridegroom decks himself with a garland, and as a bride adorns herself with her jewels. (Isaiah 61:10)

The being clothed with righteousness is related in the New Testament to the atonement of Christ. When the righteousness of Christ is imputed to the believer, the believer is no longer naked. Paul alludes to the psalmist when he writes,

"Blessed are those whose lawless deeds have been forgiven, and whose sins have been covered" (Romans 4:7).

The ultimate "covering" of the believer is anticipated by Paul as he contemplates the future status of the redeemed.

For we know that if the earthly tent which is our house is torn down, we have a building from God, a house not made with hands, eternal in the heavens. For indeed in this house we groan, longing to be clothed with our dwelling from heaven; inasmuch as we, having put it on, shall not be found naked. For indeed while we are in this tent, we groan, being burdened, because we do not want to be unclothed, but to be clothed, in order that what is mortal may be swallowed up by life. (2 Corinthians 5:1-4)

Here the ultimate hope of the New Testament is expressed—the hope of final covering, of permanent clothing. The hope of the redeemed is to be freed from the threat of nakedness and to enjoy freely the gaze of God.

Kierkegaard understood the "covering dimension" of Christ. He celebrates in passionate terms the covering provided by Christ for His people.

Oh, sure hiding-place for sinners! Oh, blessed hiding-place!—especially if one has first learned what it means when conscience accuses, and the Law condemns, and justice pursues with punishment, and then, when wearied unto despair, to find repose in the one shelter that is to be found! A man, even the most loving man, can at the most give thee extenuation and excuse, leaving it to thee to make what use of them thou art able; but himself he cannot give thee, that only Jesus Christ can do; He gives thee Himself as a shelter; it is not some comforting thought He gives thee: no, He gives thee Himself. As the night spreads concealment over everything, so did He give up His life and become a covering behind which lies a sinful world which He has saved. Through this covering justice does not break as the sun's rays break through colored glass, merely softened by refraction; no, it impotently breaks against this covering, is reflected from it and does not pass through it. He gave Himself as a covering for the whole world, for thee as well, and for me.[15]

Is it any wonder that such a God is intimidating to man? Kierkegaard's words are words of comfort, yet there is no getting around the fact that God can bless us and cover us with His love. We must be seen—completely—by Him. Sartre was right when he spoke of the awkward position man is in if he is observed by God. But Sartre's argument has little to say about whether this "Unviewed Viewer" actually exists. It has much to say about the mind of Sartre and others who, living on wishful thinking, deny the reality of the God whose gaze they cannot escape.

NOTES

1. W. Luijpen, *Fenomenologie en Atheisme* (Utrecht: Aula-Boeken, 1967), 33.
2. Jean-Paul Sartre, *Being and Nothingness,* trans. Hazel E. Barnes (New York: Washington Square, 1953), 319.
3. Ibid., 354.
4. Ibid., 355.
5. Jean-Paul Sartre, *"No Exit" and Three Other Plays* (New York: Vintage, 1949), 47.
6. Ibid.
7. Julius Fast, *Body Language* (New York: M. Evans, 1970), 140.
8. Søren Kierkegaard, *Either/Or,* vol. 2, trans. Walter Lowrie (Garden City, N.Y.: Doubleday Anchor, 1959), 163.
9. Ibid., 164.
10. Søren Kierkegaard, *"Fear and Trembling" and "The Sickness unto Death,"* trans. Walter Lowrie (Garden City, N.Y.: Doubleday Anchor, 1954), 197-198.
11. S. U. Zuidema, *Kierkegaard,* trans. David H. Freeman (Philadelphia: Presbyterian & Reformed, 1960), 20.
12. Albrecht Oepke, *"gumnos,"* vol. 1 of the *Theological Dictionary of the New Testament,* ed. Gerhard Kittel and Gerhard Friedrich, trans. Geoffrey W. Bromiley (Grand Rapids: Eerdmans, 1971), 190.
13. Martin Luther, *Lectures on Genesis,* vol. 1 of *Luther's Works,* ed. Jaroslav Pelikan (St. Louis: Concordia, 1958), 167.
14. Sartre, *Being and Nothingness,* 354.
15. Robert Bretall, ed., *A Kierkegaard Anthology* (New York: Modern Library, 1936), 424-425.

CHAPTER 7
THE HUMAN QUEST
FOR AUTONOMY

In the early sixties an Anglican priest arrived in the United States on his first visit to America. Visiting Philadelphia, he spent an afternoon browsing in antique shops, taking special note of Revolutionary Period memorabilia. He was suddenly struck by a time-worn sign hanging in a musty shop bearing the inscription of a Revolutionary War slogan:

We Serve No Sovereign Here!

He found in this a symbol of the American view of freedom, a view that carries with it a built-in repugnance toward any notion of sovereign authority. A nation that cherishes liberty above all things, preferring death to its loss, must indeed struggle with any notion that involves absolute sovereignty of anyone, including God. A central motif of the New Testament, the *kingdom* of God, is a concept alien to basic American thinking. A monarchy, even with Christ on the throne, threatens our basic principles of democracy.

Perhaps the aversion to sovereignty that is so integral to the American mentality partially explains the tendency in

American church life to relegate Christianity to an isolated "spiritual" or "religious" sphere of national life. There seems to be a process of systematic containment by which the sphere of God's authority is safely restricted to one day in the week and one institution in the culture. To be a nation "under God" does not include the idea that the political leaders are under the authority of God. Separation of church and state means more than a division of labor between two earthly institutions called to serve God in two different spheres. Rather, it has come to mean separation of state and God. Consequently, God's authority is limited to the "hearts" of religious people. A political tokenism is shown when the hats of state are doffed to the Deity in campaign speeches, inauguration ceremonies, special worship services in the White House, and state funerals. Government creeds and public statements openly acknowledge the existence of God, but acknowledgment of His sovereign authority is systematically avoided, being relegated to the sphere of the church. God's sovereignty is not boldly declared at the Supreme Court or in the Senate. The only kingdom our nation would bear would be one that was ruled by referendum. The power of veto does not belong to God. His authority is not sovereign, but must be submitted to the tribunal of the popular opinion poll. The legislation of the United States is not determined by an attempt to reflect divine principles of justice and righteousness, but by an attempt to appease various lobby groups working to protect vested interests. As Will Durant characterized Aristotle's God as a "Do-nothing" King who reigned but did not rule, so American culture wills a God who reigns in name but is not truly Sovereign.

Even within circles of religious evangelism we see an emphasis on the Christ as Savior rather than Christ as Lord. The call to repentance is called an "invitation." Where God sovereignly demands repentance and submission to the authority of His Christ, the evangelist politely "invites" people to repent. An "invitation" carries with it the right to refuse with impunity. An invitation presents an option, not an obligation, an opportunity, not a duty. But God's commands carry no RSVP—man indeed has the *power* to refuse the divine summons, but not the *right*.

Within American culture, the notion of divine sovereignty is short-circuited not only within the secular sphere, but in the religious sphere as well. God does not rule by executive privilege but must look to the populace to advise and consent. Where Protestant Christianity once risked the end of all Christian unity over the issue of *Sola Scriptura,* wherein God's authority in Scripture was to reign supreme, there now exists a profound antipathy to such authority. The liberal seminary professor cries "academic freedom" as the justification for departure from confessional standards, and the church official appeals to the "living tradition of the church" as a euphemism for dissolving biblical mandates. Where the authority of the apostle Paul was once viewed as an authority that rested upon divine sanction, it is now challenged as being merely the expression of a first-century male chauvinist. Paul is viewed by many feminists as an insufferable obstacle to women seeking "liberation." In a word, modern "liberation" involves a revolt against the sovereign authority of God as members of church and state join forces in a mutual act of cosmic treason.

When we search for influencing factors which have contributed to the breakdown of respect for divine authority, we must consider the impact of European existentialism upon our culture. Serious work in the area of human freedom and authority has been done by men such as Nietzsche, Sartre, Camus, Heidegger, and others.

FRIEDRICH NIETZSCHE AND FREEDOM

Nietzsche's conflict with Christianity often focused on Christian morality. At no point in his critique of Christendom did he become more openly hostile than at the point of morality. He saw in the legacy of the "slave morality" of Christianity the roots of the decadence that plagued his age. He says,

"Not their love, but the impotence of their love keeps today's Christians from burning us at the stake."[1] Again he writes, "Christianity gave Eros poison to drink; he did not die of it but degenerated into vice."[2] The Christian ethic with its emphasis on meekness and compassion has robbed man of the free expression of his will-to-power, producing what Nietzsche calls a "slave morality." There is no God who protects the weak and insures justice, but man still claims he exists, thus making weakness seem blessed. But since this God does not really exist, why should weakness and meekness be applauded? Nietzsche maintained the thesis made popular by Dostoevsky: If there is no God, anything is permitted! Paul Roubiczek comments,

> In The Possessed [by Dostoevsky] Kirillov is convinced that there is no God, and concludes: "If God exists, all is His will and from His will I cannot escape. If not, it's all my will and I am bound to show self-will. . . . If there is no god, then I am God." Or, as Nietzsche puts it: "If there were gods, how could I bear it to be no god myself? Therefore, there are no gods. . . ." Man, deprived of the divine, is bound to reach out for powers once considered divine.[3]

To fill the void of a universe without God, a universe which is characterized by the total rejection of tradition, morality, and authority (nihilism), Nietzsche puts forward the option of "biological heroism." Where there are no values, man must create his own. Freedom is not found in conforming to a slave morality. Master morality is achieved by the moral pioneer who lives in courage. Nietzsche says of the pioneer,

> For, believe me!—the secret of the greatest fruitfulness and the greatest enjoyment of being is: to live dangerously! Build your cities on the slopes of Vesuvius! Send your ships into unmapped seas! Live at war with your peers and with yourselves. Be robbers and conquerors, as long as you cannot be rulers and owners, you lovers of knowledge! The time is

*soon past when it will be enough for you to live hidden like
timid deer in the woods. Finally the pursuit of knowledge
will stretch out for its due; it will want to rule and possess,
and you along with it.*[4]

The pioneer spirit reaches its apex in Nietzsche's figure of
the *Übermensch,* the "superman." The superman overcomes
and supersedes the present weaknesses of inauthentic man.
He does not live in subjection to the dictates of Another, but
in his quest for autonomy he creates his own values. He
exchanges the "slave morality" of decadent Christianity for
his own "master morality." There can be no peaceful coexist-
ence between the superman and historic Christianity. In
Nietzsche's system, the existence of God would be prohibitive
for the achieving of authentic existence. The Christian God
represents the "kryptonite" that would be fatal to the superman. The Christian God must die lest He continue to cas-
trate the potentially authentic man. We read in *Thus Spake
Zarathustra,*

*And this is the great noontide: it is when man stands at
the middle of his course between animal and superman
and celebrates his journey to a new morning. . . . Then
man, going under, will bless himself; for he will be going
over to superman; and the sun of his knowledge will stand
at noontide. "All gods are dead: now we want the superman to live"—let this be our will one day at the great noontide!*[5]

Thus Christianity with its ethic of theonomy, the rule of
God, is on a collision course with man's dream of autonomy,
self-rule. If God exists, man cannot be a law unto himself. If
God exists, man's will-to-power is destined to run head-on
into the will of God. God's sovereignty looms as an invincible
threat to the aspirations of superman. If man is to be free in
the sense of autonomy, then God must die.

Nietzsche's personal attitude toward the existence of God

has been the point of countless discussions. Again we find a certain tormented ambivalence in the anguish of Nietzsche's life. At an early age he composed a poem "To the Unknown God" in which he says:

I must know thee, Unknown One, Thou who searchest out the depths of my soul, And blowest like a storm through my life. Thou art inconceivable and yet my kinsman! I must know thee and ever serve thee.[6]

In his youth Nietzsche cried out to serve God. It is obvious that this feeling haunted Nietzsche to his grave. His philosophical writings betray a pathetic struggle of "kicking against the ox-goad" that ends in the delusion of self-identity with Christ. He titles his nost autobiographical work *Ecce Homo—"Behold the Man!"* borrowing the words Pontius Pilate used to indicate Christ. After his mental breakdown, Nietzsche signed his letters "the Crucified One." For Frederick Nietzsche the quest for autonomy ended in insanity. He sent his ship into unmapped seas and found shipwreck. He built his house on the slopes of Vesuvius and was consumed by the volcano.

JEAN-PAUL SARTRE AND AUTONOMY

Where Nietzscne presented a passionate, almost poetic study of autonomy, Jean-Paul Sartre presents a very analytical study of the question. The principle of subjective volition is at the heart of his understanding of existentialism. In defining what he means by the now famous slogan, "Existence precedes essence," Sartre says,

Atheistic existentialism, which I represent, is more coherent. It states that if God does not exist, there is at least one being in whom existence precedes essence, a being who exists before he can be defined by any concept, and that this being is man, or, as Heidegger says, human reality. What is

meant here by saying that existence precedes essence? It
means that, first of all, man exists, turns up, appears on
the scene, and, only afterwards, defines himself. If man, as
the existentialist conceives him, is indefinable, it is because
at first he is nothing. Only afterward will he be something,
and he himself will have made what he will be. Thus, there
is no human nature, since there is no God to conceive it.
Not only is man what he conceives himself to be, he is only
what he wills himself to be after this thrust toward exis-
tence.[7]

For Sartre the first principle of existentialism is that "man
is nothing else but what he makes of himself."[8] Man is
autonomous. He must choose what he chooses by himself.
This involves, of course, an awesome burden of responsibility.
In self-choice, man is choosing for all mankind. His decision is
not done in isolation.

In fact, in creating the man that we want to be, there is not
a single one of our acts which does not at the same time
create an image of man as we think he ought to be.[9]

Sartre was serious about the burden or responsibility that
attends decision. It is the burden of God. The loss of God he
called distressing, and he had little time for classical humanis-
tic ethics that seek to maintain the values and norms of
Christianity without their ultimate foundation, God. Man is
free with the absence of God, but this freedom Sartre views
as man's condemnation.

If God does not exist, we find no values or commands to
turn to which legitimize our conduct. So, in the bright
realm of values, we have no excuse behind us, nor justifica-
tion before us. We are alone, with no excuses.[10]

At times Sartre seems to celebrate man's freedom in
autonomy, and at other times he laments it. In his play *The*

Flies, Sartre does not seem so distressed about the absence of God. Rather, the God Zeus, presented as a disgusting god of flies, appears as the menacing threat to human freedom. When Orestes rebels from the "flock" of Zeus, Zeus calls him back by threatening him with exile if he refuses to return and promising him peace if he does return. Orestes replies,

Foreign to myself—I know it. Outside nature, against nature, without excuse, beyond remedy, except what remedy I find within myself. But I shall not return under your law; I am doomed to have no other law but mine. Nor shall I come back to nature, the nature you found good; in it are a thousand beaten paths all leading up to you—but I must blaze my trail. For I, Zeus, am a man, and every man must find out his own way. Nature abhors man, and you too, god of gods, abhor mankind.[11]

Here Orestes declares his magna charta. He defies the authority of Zeus. He sees his declaration of autonomy as sealing his own doom. "I am doomed to have no other law but mine." Condemned to be free, Orestes does not delight in his autonomy. He is not like an adolescent who becomes giddy over the relaxation of rules. Freedom is a burden, but he prefers the doom of autonomy over submission to Zeus. He may find this freedom unpleasant, but not as unpleasant as coming under the rule of Zeus. Zeus is powerless to prevent Orestes' self-emancipation. He shares the "secret of the gods" with Aegisthus:

Once freedom lights its beacon in a man's heart, the gods are powerless against him. It's a matter between man and man, and it is for other men, and for them only, to let him go his gait, or to throttle him.[12]

For Sartre, God represents a threat to authentic morality. If God is autonomous, then man cannot be. By rejecting the existence of God, Sartre claims that he makes room for real freedom and morality. He argues that the rejection of God makes morality possible. W. Luijpen, the Dutch Catholic scholar, raises the question, "Perhaps it is Sartre's morality that makes the rejection of God necessary."[13]

Although there are decisive differences between Nietzsche and Sartre as well as between Albert Camus, Martin Heidegger, and other existentialist writers, a similar strain of moral autonomy versus the sovereignty of God is evident in all of them. For Heidegger, being is authentic only when it manifests itself through self-determination and self-projection. Man, in experiencing the "thrownness" of his existence *(Geworfenheit)*, hangs suspended between past and future. To overcome the anxiety that this situation produces, he must carve out his own destiny. Authentic existence is characterized by a freedom that can only be maintained apart from heteronomy.[14]

Thus, atheistic existentialism, with its view of autonomous human freedom, inevitably places itself in opposition to Christianity. Its understanding of man makes the God-hypothesis of classical theism untenable. Of course, no one can refute the argument that the sovereignty of God and the autonomy of man are irreconcilable polar opposites. Surely the atheist is correct in asserting that full human autonomy is incompatible with divine sovereignty.

However, though there is tacit agreement between atheism and historic Christianity at this point, the Christian must go on to pose several questions. Not least is the question whether one can be autonomous simply because he declares himself to be. Ultimately, man can be completely autonomous only if, indeed, there is no God. Atheists argue for the nonexistence of God using the premise that such a God cannot be because man is autonomous. But this in turn can be demonstrated only if it is first known that God does not exist. To say this is to argue from the center of a most vicious circle. (One could also raise the question of whether any individual can be autonomous in a world where various kinds of human authority inevitably cramp the style of self-rule.)

Atheistic existentialism also makes the assertion—but cannot demonstrate—that moral autonomy is a necessary prerequisite for freedom. The fact that man is a volitional being, a being with a will of his own, is indeed crucial to his being a man and not a thing, a subject and not an object. But must volition be raised to the level of autonomy to be regarded as free? Is it not possible that we could possess free will and still be under the rule of God?

BIBLICAL VIEW OF FREEDOM AND AUTONOMY

In biblical categories of free will, man is created within a framework of freedom, but not autonomy. Man is given freedom, but is refused autonomy. Full autonomy belongs to God alone. Man's freedom is within limits. In the Eden situation he enjoys freedom, but it is not unlimited freedom.

The LORD God took the man and put him into the garden of Eden to cultivate it and keep it. And the LORD God commanded the man, saying, "From any tree of the garden you may eat freely; but from the tree of knowledge of good and evil you shall not eat, for in the day that you eat from it you shall surely die." (Genesis 2:15-17)

God places man in a garden paradise. Man's role is not that of a slave with no freedom or authority but of one who is given dominion over the earth. Man functions as God's vassal being or vice-regent over all creation. Freedom is his, but with one restriction placed upon him: Man is free and responsible, but he is responsible to the law of God.

The biblical narrative of the Fall rehearses the original quest for autonomy.

Now the serpent was more crafty than any beast of the field which the LORD God had made. And he said to the woman, "Indeed, has God said, 'You shall not eat from any tree of the garden'?" And the woman said to the serpent, "From the fruit of the trees of the garden we may eat; but from the fruit of the tree which is in the middle of the garden, God has said, 'You shall not eat from it or touch it, lest you die.'" And the serpent said to the woman, "You surely shall not die. For God knows that in the day you eat from it your eyes will be opened, and you will be like God, knowing good and evil." When the woman saw that the tree was good for food, and that it was a delight to the eyes, and that the tree was desirable to make one wise, she took from its fruit and ate; and she gave also to her husband with her, and he ate. (Genesis 3:1-6)

The seduction scene begins with a crafty question, "Did God say?" The serpent raises a question about the limits imposed upon Adam and Eve's freedom. In the very question there is a hint of mockery of the divine command. The implied suggestion is that it was unworthy of God to so restrict His creatures. Martin Luther comments on the text,

Here properly belong these words: "Did God actually command you?" This is an instance of the awful boldness of the devil, as he invents a new god and denies the former true and eternal God with such unconcern and assurance. It is as if he were to say: "Surely you are silly if you believe that God has given such a command, for it is not God's nature to be so deeply concerned whether you eat or not. Inasmuch as it is the tree of the knowledge of good and evil, how can such ill will come upon Him that He does not want you to be wise?"[15]

The integrity of God is called into question by the serpent. Not only does the serpent raise questions about what God said, but he asks the question in such a way as to distort the commandment. He says, "Has God said, 'You shall not eat from any tree in the garden'?" The serpent obviously knew very well that God had not put the whole garden off limits. The distortion implies the notion that without autonomy there is no freedom. When Eve becomes defensive, protesting their liberty, the serpent becomes boldly direct. He now flatly contradicts the warning of God, saying, "You surely shall not die." The bold and arrogant assertion of the serpent declares to Eve that she can disobey God with impunity. He suggests, like Orestes, that God is powerless to carry out His threat. You are responsible to no one is clearly implied in the statement.

Then comes the serpentine promise, the promise of blessing that goes with autonomy, *Sicut erat dei*—"You will be as god!" This is the essence of the primordial temptation—to be like God, to have no restraints, no limits, no crowding of self-desire by the rule of another. To be autonomous—that's the temptation.

The irony of humanism, which seeks the deification of man, is that it has its origin not in the creed of the ancient agnostic philosopher Protagoras, *Homo mensura* ("Man is the measure of all things"), but in the promise of a serpent, *Sicut erat dei*. Humanism was not invented by man, but by a snake who suggested that the quest for autonomy might be a good idea.

The promise of the serpent was not fulfilled. Adam and Eve did not become gods. Autonomy was not found. What followed was a tragic loss of the freedom previously enjoyed. Human freedom was not augmented, but diminished by the Fall. The quest for autonomy, however, did not cease. It continues even to this day, east and west of Eden.

The quest for autonomy elucidated in the narrative of the Fall takes on larger dimensions in the mind of the psalmist. In Psalm 2 the writer envisions a conspiracy, not of one man and one woman, but of the aggregate forces of the political kingdoms of this world. The psalmist asks:

Why are the nations in an uproar, and the peoples devising a vain thing? The kings of the earth take their stand, and the rulers take counsel together against the LORD and against His Anointed: "Let us tear their fetters apart, and cast away their cords from us!" (Psalm 2:1-3)

The psalm begins with a rhetorical question, a question that suggests amazement at such a manifestation of arrogance and folly. The scene depicts a massive conspiracy to overthrow the authority of God and His Anointed One. (Taken historically, the "Anointed" would refer to the established king of Israel; taken prophetically, to the Messiah, the Christ.) The nations are in a state of tumultuous uproar and are amazed. This rage is manifested in a summit meeting at which the kings and rulers of the world lay aside their paltry differences to join forces against a common enemy. Their border disputes become insignificant as they resolve together to unite their power against the supreme threat, the sovereignty of God.

Why the hostility? Why do the kings rattle their swords in belligerence? The answer is obvious: They despise the rule of God, for it restricts their freedom. Again, the goal is autonomy. The rule of God is regarded as ropes and chains binding them and keeping them from unbridled pursuance of their desire. So the secret weapons are unveiled, the battleships come out of dry dock, the nuclear stockpile is tapped, and the troops are mobilized as the whole world joins the cosmic liberation movement. With the infantile resolve of the child who seeks to quench a blazing fire with a piece of straw, the rulers set themselves against the sovereignty of God.

The response of the Lord God to this revolution is not unconditional surrender; it is not a flurry of actions born of panic; it is not a desperate plea for negotiation in the context of a guarded truce. Rather, "The one who sits in the heavens laughs." He is temporarily amused by this act of collective insanity. But His laughter turns to anger as He mobilizes His own power to vindicate His Anointed.

Throughout biblical history we see repeated acts of rebellion against God's sovereign authority. The consequence of these acts is the consequence of the Fall. God punishes with poetic justice. His punishment is in kind. The quest for autonomy produces not liberation, but the loss of freedom. The New Testament describes fallen man as being in bondage, a slave to his own passions.

If ever there is a genuine paradox to be found in Holy Writ, it is at the point of freedom and bondage. The paradox is this: When one seeks to rebel from God, he gains only bondage. When he becomes a slave to God, he becomes free. Liberty is found in obedience. The Anglican poet John Donne understood this when he wrote in a sonnet,

Except You enthrall me, never shall I be free.

Jesus provoked the wrath of the Pharisees by saying, "If you abide in My word, then you are truly disciples of Mine; and you shall know the truth, and the truth shall make you free" (John 8:31-32). The offer of freedom by Jesus did not effect a chorus of hosannas. The Pharisees were insulted, arguing that they were already free and hardly needed liberation. Jesus replied, "Truly, truly, I say to you, every one who commits sin is the slave of sin" (John 8:34). Jesus located human slavery in the bondage of the self to its own evil desires. He counters their protestations with the statement, "If therefore the Son shall make you free, you shall be free indeed" (John 8:36).

The apostle Paul elaborates this theme in his Letter to the Romans:

For if we have become united with Him in the likeness of His death, certainly we shall be also in the likeness of His resurrection, knowing this, that our old self was crucified with Him, that our body of sin might be done away with, that we should no longer be slaves to sin; for he who has died is freed from sin. (Romans 6:5-7)

Here the apostle indicates "irreconcilable differences" with the Pharisees. The Pharisees sought freedom by living for the Law and crucifying Christ. Paul found liberty by crucifying the Law and living for Christ.

Do you not know that when you present yourselves to someone as slaves for obedience, you are slaves of the one whom

you obey, either of sin resulting in death, or of obedience re-
sulting in righteousness? But thanks be to God that though
you were slaves of sin, you became obedient from the heart
to that form of teaching to which you were committed, and
having been freed from sin, you became slaves of righteous-
ness. (Romans 6:16-18)

For Paul, there is no liberty in rebellion, only bondage. Liberty is found in obedience in the presence of the Lord. He concludes, "Now the Lord is the Spirit; and where the Spirit of the Lord is, there is liberty" (2 Corinthians 3:17).

The biblical God remains a massive threat to illusions of moral autonomy. The result is that even though a man may be convinced of the truth of God's existence, that intellectual assertion in itself could not overcome the moral inclination to flee from that truth. Man's corruption is such that he will do everything in his power to disprove, combat, obscure, and deny the truth of that knowledge.

NOTES
1. Houston Peterson, ed., *Essays in Philosophy* (New York: Pocket Books, 1959) 220.
2. Ibid., 228.
3. Paul Roubiczek, *Existentialism For and Against* (Cambridge: Cambridge University Press, 1964), 32.
4. Robert N. Beck, ed., *Perspectives on Philosophy* (New York: Holt, Rinehart & Winston, 1961), 371.
5. Friedrich Nietzsche, *Thus Spake Zarathustra*, trans. R. J. Hollingdale (Baltimore: Penguin, 1961), 104.
6. Cited by William Barrett in *Irrational Man* (Garden City, N.Y.: Doubleday Anchor, 1958), 186.
7. Beck, *Perspectives on Philosophy,* 371.
8. Ibid.
9. Ibid.
10. Ibid., 366.
11. Jean-Paul Sartre, *"No Exit" and Three Other Plays* (New York: Vintage, 1949), 122.
12. Ibid., 104.
13. W. Luijpen, *Fenomenologie en Atheisme* (Utrecht: Aula-Boeken, 1967), 32.
14. Cf. my article "Existential Autonomy and Christian Freedom," *Christianity Today,* 18 July 1969, 13.
15. Martin Luther, *Lectures on Genesis,* vol. 1 of *Luther's Works,* ed. Jaroslav Pelikan (St. Louis: Concordia, 1958), 149.

CONCLUSION
THE NEVER-ENDING BIAS

In 1736, in Northampton, Massachusetts, Jonathan Edwards preached a sermon titled "Men Are Naturally God's Enemies." In this sermon, Edwards gave a lengthy exposition of the biblical text, "For if when we were enemies, we were reconciled to God by the death of His Son" (Romans 5:10). The basic thesis of the sermon was that man hated God. Edwards allowed that men rarely claim moral perfection and would readily admit that they sinned. However, men protest the charge that they are enemies of God, arguing that they bear no malice and feel no hatred toward God. Edwards proceeded to analyze human behavior in such a way as to demonstrate that man shows his hostility to God by his behavior.

They are enemies in the natural relish of their souls. They have an inbred distaste and disrelish of God's perfections. God is not such a sort of being as they would have. Though they are ignorant of God, yet from what they hear of Him, and from what is manifest by the light of nature of God, they do not like Him. By His being endowed with such attributes as He is, they have an aversion to Him. They hear God is an infinitely holy, pure, and righteous Being, and they do not like Him upon this account; they have no relish

*of such kind of qualifications; they take no delight in con-
templating them. It would be a mere task, a bondage to a
natural man, to be obliged to set himself to contemplate
these attributes of God. They see no manner of beauty or lo-
veliness nor taste any sweetness in them. And upon the account of their distaste of these perfections, they dislike all
the other of His attributes. They have greater aversion to
Him because He is omniscient and knows all things; because His omniscience is a holy omniscience. They are not
pleased that He is omnipotent, and can do whatever He
pleases; because it is a holy omnipotence. They are enemies
even to His mercy, because it is a holy mercy. They do not
like His immutability, because by this He never will be otherwise than He is, an infinitely holy God.[1]*

The thesis of this book is in substantial agreement with
Edwards's analysis of man's disposition toward God. The
theme is that natural man suffers from prejudice. He operates
within a framework of insufferable bias against the God of
Christianity. The Christian God is utterly repugnant to him
because He represents the threat of threats to man's own desires and ambitions. The will of man is on a collision course
with the will of God. Such a course leads inevitably to a conflict of interests.

There is no dispute with Freud, Nietzsche, and Marx on
the issue of man's ability to create a god according to his
own psychological desire or need. This is precisely what
biblical Christianity asserts is the case. There is no dispute
that gods so created will reflect the desires of the human
creators, as Feuerbach maintained. The dispute, of course, is
located in the question of whether men would be naturally
disposed to create the Christian God. Though it is freely acknowledged and granted that man would be pleased to receive the benefits that only God could give them, it is highly
questionable whether men desire the God who makes those
benefits possible. Men would apparently rather die in their
sin than live forever in obedience. (In John Milton's *Paradise*

Lost, Satan states that it is "Better to reign in hell than serve in heaven.") They would rather hide behind trees than face the penetrating gaze of God. They would prefer moral anarchy to the law of God.

The writer is grateful to the labor of Marx, Freud, Nietzsche, Sartre, and Feuerbach for their exposé of the idols fabricated by men. In this respect they have done a worthy service to Christianity. Perhaps their iconoclasm will penetrate into those churches which participate in the systematic distortion of the Christian God. So great is the tendency toward idolatry that even the Christian who knows grace must continue to struggle against the negative inclinations of his old nature. Can the wholesale attack on the authority of Scripture in our day represent merely the "assured results of higher criticism," or does the modern church betray a delight in disposing of the weight of biblical authority? Does the question of the existence of God present problems that are ultimately intellectual or moral?

These questions must be faced before any serious intellectual effort can be made regarding Christian truth claims. I must always ask myself, Do I believe what I believe because I am honestly persuaded by cogent reasoning that it is true, or do I believe what I believe merely because in the final analysis that's what I *want* to believe? If I say I am a Christian, do I believe in the God revealed in Scripture, or do I participate in a systematic distortion of that God to suit my own desires? Do I believe in the God who is, or do I believe in a god of my own creation?

The question of the existence of and nature of God is a question attended by a host of vested interests. If we are to examine the question with integrity, we must both recognize and face the implications of our vested interests. If we refuse to do that, then truth will perish, and so will we.

NOTE

1. Jonathan Edwards, *The Works of President Edwards,* vol. 4 (New York: Robert Carter and Brothers, 1879), 38.

INDEX OF NAMES